Contents

INTRODUCTION

The European Union has been largely presented by British politicians as an economic bargain for the UK. The UK joined when it was in economic decline and seeking access to the growing markets of the Continent and was prepared to sacrifice its preferential relationship with the Commonwealth. Eventually, under Thatcher, Britain relinquished its status as the sick man of Europe and was able to prosper and encourage two key EU developments in the single market reforms and the expansion into the former soviet bloc nations. UK politicians may have recognised the economic perils of the euro, but the City was a major beneficiary from the integrated capital markets and capital flows that resulted. The Great Recession from 2008 was viewed by the Brussels elite as a crisis of Anglo Saxon capitalism and confirmed their suspicion of loosely regulated markets, but it shortly became more a crisis of the Eurozone and the inability of the EU institutions and the Eurozone nations to agree collective and effective policy responses. France and Germany have driven much of the EU's integration, but are now on opposite sides of the economic debate, with France and others struggling to introduce necessary economic reforms. In the words of Pope Francis when addressing the European Parliament in November 2014, the institution was "elderly and haggard" driven by an "inhumane" spirit and swamped by "bureaucratic technicalities".[1]

In 2015 the UK is exhibiting strong growth and much reduced unemployment, while the Euro area continues to perform weakly. Even with the benefit of the current gentle recovery and quantitative easing, unemployment in the Eurozone is forecast by the ECB to be 10 % in 2017. There are concerns that the Eurozone is becoming the new Japan, but without the social cohesiveness of that society to manage the human and social costs. Over the past 20 years Italy has demonstrated virtually no growth, with only Zimbabwe and Haiti performing worse. Italian and Spanish youth unemployment is above 40%. Nationalism has flourished as a result of insecurity. In Italy the three major opposition parties are all anti Euro. Even in Germany the anti Euro party, AfD are making breakthroughs and in France Marine Le Pen of the far right Front National that is calling for EU withdrawal, is a leading candidate to be the next President.

Roger Bootle has summarised the political and economic philosophy of European integration[2] as

- The means to avoid another European War.
- That it is natural for Europe to be united.
- In economics and politics size really matters.
- Europe needs to be united to resist the competitive challenge from Asia.

However today the EU is widely acknowledged even by its supporters as a malfunctioning political unit. Its philosophy reflects the era of large blocs before globalisation, the rise of emerging markets and the growth in the number of independent nations. Unlike national politics the EU has, to date, had no pendulum, but only one direction of greater powers and integration without any ability to "throw the rascals out". In the words of Fukuyama "political accountability provides a peaceful path towards institutional adaption"[3] and the EU is struggling for that legitimacy as it has expanded its powers. Moreover, the EU has undertaken greater integration while undertaking a huge expansion in membership into very different political and economic cultures. The north-south conflicts produced by the euro crisis, the global competitive challenges faced, the long term unfavourable demographic and "social Europe" public debt trends are all now producing forces which will mean

[1] Pope Francis, *Speech to European Parliament,* 25 November 2014
[2]Bootle, Roger, *The Trouble with Europe*, London, 2014, p. 16

[3] Fukuyama, *The Origins of Political Order,* London, 2011, p. 483

the EU will be greatly challenged to survive in its present form. This critique of the EU must be balanced by the fact that in integrating firstly the new democracies of Southern Europe and later those in Eastern Europe, it has contributed to the peace, security and improved prosperity for those nations. Indeed the Ukraine crisis has emphasised the critical importance of the EU to Eastern European members, (albeit we will see that EU policy contributed to the crisis). But could not much of this been achieved without the European integration ideology? In Eastern Europe there is evidence of a return to the older politics and power bases before membership in some nations such as Hungary. More widely, tensions arising from the Euro and other issues such as migration, are reinforcing the dominance of national political interests.

In the UK Euroscepticism, or outright hostility, have consistently been well represented in the British attitude to the EU. The rise of UKIP and the political focus on immigration has moved the question of the UK's relationship up the political agenda. The Conservative government elected in May 2015 now seeks to renegotiate the UK's relationship with the EU before holding an "In-Out" referendum. A recent Populus UK poll indicated that 39 % were in favour of leaving the EU and 41 % remaining[4], indicating a high level of uncertainty as to the eventual result.

A review of the costs and benefits of the EU is therefore timely, particularly as the political argument has difficulty progressing beyond pro Europeans warning of the dark abyss of leaving, while the anti Europeans envisage only the sunny uplands of global free trade and markets, combined sometimes with immigration controls. This paper will trace the evolution of the EU and the UK's relationship and attitude to it over time. It will examine how the integration project has evolved and then analyse economic, democratic and geopolitical implications for the UK. It is a story where most of the UK's political class seem to have discounted the ultimate objectives of the EU and where a pattern can be identified where the UK has enthusiastically supported certain aspects of EU integration, but has then been surprised by the eventual implications. In the words of Janan Ganesh, "since the beginning, nothing has wounded British interests more than our idle hope that Europe is not serious about unity."[5]

This paper concludes at the Conservative general election victory and before renegotiation negotiations were begun. The unexpected strength of David Cameron's mandate had surprised the EU, the migration crisis has yet to intensify.

---

[4] Pickard, Jim, "Britons split on EU exit, says poll" in *Financial Times,* 15 April 2015
[5] Ganesh, Janan, *From a reluctant European: A memo to the PM*, London, 2015, p. 6

Sources

The research for this paper has been undertaken primarily utilising:

- The research output, commentary and public meetings of think tanks and pressure groups such as Open Europe, The Bruges Group, Business for Britain, Bruegel, The CBI, The Centre for European Reform and Chatham House.
- Reports of Parliamentary committees and the UK Government's review of EU Competencies.
- Political memoirs and recently published critiques of the European Union.
- Newspaper analysis and commentary.

A SHORT HISTORY OF THE EU

In order to appreciate the UK's relationship with the EU it is necessary to outline its development and recognise it was a political project from conception. Indeed its role (along others) in ensuring that a major Western European conflict is now unthinkable and in assimilating much of Eastern Europe into the West are its clearest achievements. The EU also claims an important role in generating economic prosperity. More recent events are calling many of its achievements into question.

The Founding Fathers

The two individuals who are recognised as having played a pivotal role in establishing the foundations of European integration are the Frenchmen Robert Schuman and Jean Monnet. Monnet was appointed Head of the French Planning Commission after the war with already well established views as to the political benefits of economic integration and the formation of a European federation of states[6]. In his ambitions it would be a bloc that would not only remove the possibility of another European war, but that would stand alongside the US and the Soviet Union and provide economic and military security to Europe. This was a view adopted by Schumann who was successively Finance Minister (1946-7), Prime Minister (1947-8) and Foreign Minister (1948-52). As Foreign Minister he proposed that France and Germany place their coal and steel industries under a common authority. In May 1950 Schuman had made the "Schuman Declaration" which had been prepared by Monnet and laid out the plans for the French and German coal and steel industries. It said:

"The pooling of coal and steel production should immediately provide for the setting up of common foundations for economic development as a first step in the federation of Europe, and will change the destinies of those regions which have long been devoted to the manufacture of munitions of war, of which they have been the most constant victims."

It provided the basis for the European Coal and Steel Community (ECSC) which was formed in 1952 of the six nations, France, Germany, Belgium, Italy, Luxembourg and the Netherlands. Without the UK's involvement, Monnet dominated the negotiations for the ECSC which resolved the coal and steel conflicts between France and Germany that were the main obstacle to an economic partnership.

The major international debt relief that Germany obtained in 1953 was also highly significant for Germany and Europe's economic revival. In 2015, some contrast with Germany's own attitude as a creditor to the indebtedness of Greece and others, that can be seen struggling from the debts arising from the euro's failures.

The momentum for moving quickly onward to the EEC arose from the French National Assembly's rejection in 1954 of a plan to develop a supranational European army (EDC) including West Germany to counter the Soviet threat. This seems today a very ambitious objective and it saw the UK's cynicism vindicated, sent a shock wave through the six and undermined Monnet's "spillover" view of European integration[78]. However, to regain momentum the Belgian Foreign Minister organised a

---

[6] A veteran of Verdun, his ideas were published in 1929 as "The United States of Europe idea" while serving at the League of Nations.

[7] Blair, Alasdair, *The European Union*, London, 2012, p. 31.

[8] Best, Heinrich et al, *The Europe of Elites*, London, 2012, p. 2, "Spillover" is a term used in the influential functional integration theory that was developed in the late 1950's. Once integration has been initiated in one sector it spills over to others and from the economic to the political sphere. Thus the integration processes acquire a logic of their own and reinforce themselves.

meeting at the Italian port of Messina from which the "Messina Declaration "set the course for the formation of the EEC and atomic energy community.

The EEC's early ambitions were modestly economic, but the preamble to the 1957 Treaty of Rome declared that the six signatories were "determined to lay the foundations of an ever closer union among the peoples of Europe ". The choice of Rome for the treaty was indeed full of deliberate symbolism. So from the very beginning the EEC was set up to become something more than it already was. To be a member was potentially to participate in a process to full integration. With three wars involving Germany since 1870 and with experience of the Second World War ingrained in the memories of all politicians, preventing another war through the development of a powerful supranational institution was a key motivator. Integration and supranationalism would diminish the nation state which had been intrinsically prone to aggressive nationalism. The establishment of the ECSC and later the EEC provided a route for Germany to re-establish its international legitimacy and also led to the reassertion of French leadership in Europe.

Securing the Foundations of the EEC

To govern the Community the Treaty of Rome maintained the same institutional design as the ECSC. The European Commission acted as an executive and as a civil service, while to balance the supranational viewpoint of the commission the views of nation states were taken into account through the creation of a Council of Ministers, a grouping of nation state ministers whose membership was determined by the subject discussed. A weak democratic element was initially provided through a Parliamentary Assembly of representatives of national parliaments. From 1979 this was replaced by direct elections to a European Parliament. Finally, because the Community is a legal body, a Court of Justice was established to interpret the treaties and decisions that had been taken.

The development of the Community is a story of the growth of the areas of competence of the Commission through Treaties and the activism (and accepted legitimacy) of the Court of Justice, together with shifting power and influence arising from the growing power of Parliament and the admission of many new nations. The combination of the growth of the policy range of the Community and the expansion of membership has inevitably led to a loss of national veto's and the pooling of sovereignty in a wide range of areas beyond an "economic community".

Key initial policies were establishing a Common Agricultural Policy and a Customs Union. Although the latter was largely achieved in goods by 1968, significant non tariff barriers, such as local standards, remained. The EEC established collective positions in international trade discussions during the 1960's. The EEC was a success. In the period 1958-70 trade among the 6 EEC members increased 5 fold. Exports to the rest of the world increased two and a half times. The GDP of members increased at an average annual rate of 5 %. [9]

The UK Conservative Government applied to join the EEC in 1961 (alongside Denmark, Ireland and Norway), partially to gain access to the strong Western European economy. However, France and Charles De Gaulle ensured that the application was not accepted, highlighting the different economic character of the UK and the agricultural support focus of the EEC budget. All new entry talks were abandoned.

In a theme we will see repeated, the expansionary aspirations of Brussels have often run ahead or conflicted with national interests. Charles de Gaulle, President of the 5th French Republic, was the dominant European figure in the 1960's. A dispute with the European Commission over the EEC obtaining its own financial resources to fund the CAP together with issues of sovereignty came up.

---

[9] Blair, A, p. 38

The latter arose from a provision of the Treaty of Rome which provided for some use of majority voting in the European Council from 1966, which was seen as not in France's interests. This resulted in 1965 in a six month French boycott of Brussels decision making known as the "empty chair crisis", which was only resolved by the so called "Luxembourg Compromise". This enabled a country to insist on unanimity of agreement where very important interests were at stake. This outcome was highly significant and swung the pendulum away for a while from the influence of the European Commission and to the nation state. The Luxembourg Compromise has not been utilised for over 40 years, although it was proffered as a protector of national sovereignty in the UK accession process. Some advocates of reform are calling for its revival today.

The European Commission's continued ambitions for deeper integration of Europe resulted in ambitious proposals in 1970 for economic and monetary union and foreign policy co operation, which were only realised decades later. A more successful area of progress was enlargement with the UK, Denmark and Ireland joining in 1973. Norway failed to join following a referendum. The oil shock crisis of the 1970's meant that nations focused on their own domestic issues which, combined with EEC institutions that were perceived as weak, meant there was little further change of significance in that decade.

The Single European Market-the driver of integration

The 1980's gave impetus for attention to Europe's poor economic performance compared with America and Japan. The practical aspects of free trade within the EEC were not functioning properly due to non tariff barriers and subsidies for domestic companies. The European domestic political agenda moved towards the support of free markets, most notably when France's Mitterand was forced by an economic crisis to abandon socialist national economic policies in 1983. Thus the European Single Market agenda was developed to create a true customs union. Led by the British European Commissioner, Sir Arthur Cockfield, nearly 300 individual measures were identified and from the passing of what became known as the Single European Act (SEA) at the 1985 Luxembourg European Council, some 280 items of legislation were adopted in the period 1986-1992, often replacing national rules with European rules.

The SEA established what became known as the Four Freedoms of the free movement of people, goods, services and capital and was the first major EEC revision since its formation. The SEA also widened the EEC's activities into new policy areas such as the environment and introduced majority voting in the Council as an inevitable requirement to ensure the single market could be implemented in the face of protectionist resistance. Most importantly, the process of creating a single market meant harmonisation of standards in a multitude of ways and meant European legislation Directives and their implementation through national laws and their enforcement by the ECJ. Particularly in the field of services this process remains incomplete to this day but, with hindsight, the SEA was much more profound in its impact than many leaders thought due to the broader and broader interpretation of the reach of Single Market measures helped by jurisprudence and subsequent treaties. For the most part national leaders failed to engage with their electorates on the issues of integration and papered over concerns about the loss of sovereignty.

The two years leading up to the SEA had also seen a restrengthening of ties between France and Germany as personified by the relationship between President Mitterrand and Chancellor Kohl. French policy was to keep the Germans fully bound into the European Community which Germany acquiesced in, as it reassured Germany's neighbours. Thatcher noted that in the two years leading up to the SEA there had been a "profound shift " in how European policy was conducted with a Franco-German block setting the agenda alongside a "tough talented federalist ", Jacques Delors.[10]

---

[10] Thatcher, Margaret, *The Downing Street Years*, London, 1993, p. 558

Jacques Delors, the former French Foreign Minister was President of the European Commission from 1985 to 1994 and reinvigorated development. In preparation for the SEA Luxembourg council he urged fulfilment of the "two great dreams for Europe of an area of no frontiers and monetary union". "Every exemption or derogation which other countries, like Britain, sought seemed to be regarded as a kind of betrayal", wrote Thatcher.[11] Other countries notably Italy and the smaller nations such as the Netherlands and Luxembourg wanted to move towards union. Jacques Santer, the Prime Minister of Luxembourg wrote to Margaret Thatcher urging an ambitious attitude and urging that the Council should "provide the starting point for the economic and psychological changes which are essential as Europe assumes its new role. The British delegation, Thatcher said, viewed these aspirations as unrealistic," where we were mistaken was in underestimating the determination of some European politicians to put them into effect ".[12] Mitterrand saw integration as an important means of preventing a Germany, that had been reunited in 1981, becoming a threat to European peace. The successful applications of Greece, Spain and Portugal in the 1980's, all considerably weaker economically than the existing members was driven by the wish to support the new democracies and also in the interests of European peace. For those states and later the countries of Eastern Europe, the EU represented a guarantee of democracy and rule of law at home, rather than a threat to their sovereignty as it is often presented in the UK.

Delors made "Social Europe "one of his priorities arguing that it had to develop alongside the Single Market to avoid companies relocating in search of reduced costs or having to aggressively restructure to reduce costs. The British and Irish refused to participate. In 1989 the European Commission published a report proposing a single currency which Delors saw as the logical conclusion to the single market.

Maastricht

With the break up of the Soviet Union and the fall of the Berlin wall, agreement was reached to look at the institutions and policies of the EEC. The result was the Maastricht Treaty of 1991 which marked a decisive move forward on integration. Agreement was reached to establish the Euro (the European Central Bank was formed in 1998), and the creation of the Social Chapter that extended the number of policy areas including health and safety and working conditions (the UK opted out at this stage). The name of the Community was changed to the European Union, the concept of the EU citizen was introduced and more co operation on foreign affairs and judicial matters was planned, albeit they remained subject to national control. It also marked a bigger role for the Parliament which would now decide legislation alongside the Council. Against the grain of the integration drive of Maastricht was the Anglo- German initiative of introducing the rule of subsidiarity to decision making. Time was to show that the concept would not be an effective break on loss of national sovereignty.

The Euro was to become the focus of European integration, but those who drove it saw it primarily as a political rather than an economic project. The Euro was partially a price Mitterrand extracted to reduce the impact of the Bundesbank in return for the unification of Germany. It was not a project popular with the German people and its political and economic implications were understood by the Bundesbank much better than most other members, who thus opposed it. According to Malcolm Rifkind, the former UK foreign secretary, Mitterrand and Kohl recognised that some sort of Euro crisis was inevitable, but expected this would produce momentum for more shared sovereignty.[13] This is indeed an enduring philosophy of the integration project, that a step forward would result from solving the crises that would inevitably result on the journey.

---

[11] Thatcher, p. 551
[12] Thatcher, p. 552
[13] Sir Malcolm Rifkind speaking at a University of Buckingham Seminar on 22 October, 2014.

The "method Monnet" and the road to integration.

Maastricht and Delors represented a tipping point in the development of the EU from more than a customs union project. From then on successive treaties enlarged the power and competency of its institutions while attempting to manage its governance issues. Its institutions have attempted to gain their own democratic legitimacy in competition to national democracies. What is remarkable about the development of the EU has been the greater pooling of sovereignty that has been achieved at the same time that membership has expanded exponentially. The pattern that has enabled this to happen has been:

- France and Germany have been consistent drivers of integration. However while, in the words of Thatcher, "the French were federalists on grounds of tactics", to curb German power, the Germans were "federalist by conviction". This was to demonstrate the new Germany would not behave as the old Germany from Bismarck to Hitler. As Germany's relative economic strength has increased this has implications, as Germany has been prepared to give more powers to the European Parliament while France preferred more national power through the Council.[14]
- Ambitious European institutions with their key actors driven by the European ideal and insulated from democratic accountability and supported by a rules based culture. A rules based culture which has proved remarkably malleable when necessary.
- Key decisions, such as monetary unification are taken initially in small steps alongside a multitude of other initiatives to minimise opposition before becoming an "inevitable" process. The ultimate objective remains ambiguous, agreements are drafted to mean different things to different nations. This is sometimes known as the "method Monnet".
- A national political class that has sought the economic, foreign and security policy benefits of pooled sovereignty while relying on ambiguity and rule bending to manage awkward aspects and in some cases convince their national electorate.
- The principle of the Four Freedoms of the Single Market has been increasingly broadly defined through treaties, the broad interpretation of Single Market measures by the ECJ and often subsequent confirming legislation, approved utilising QMV.

At least in the core nations, the populations have been increasingly less enthusiastic and when, given the opportunity through referendums have had a predisposition to reject losses of national sovereignty. Maastricht, for example, was approved in a French referendum by the smallest of margins. It is not controversial to observe that European integration has consistently been a project of an elite occurring over the heads of the populations. In the words of Monnet and reflected subsequently in the "benign despotism of enlightened leaders", "I thought it wrong to consult the peoples of Europe about the structure of a community of which they had no practical experience"[15]. The people, from a Franco-German perspective, were, after the experience of the 1930's, not to be trusted. It can be argued that the culture is more longstanding than that Robert Tombs, in an essay on Europeanism, notes that the three biggest continental countries, Germany, Italy and modern France were created by determined elites which overcame resistance and so the EU was following that example. To the disciples of ever closer union, they are the vanguard creating the European state, the final stage of an inevitable process of turning small nations into one.[16] From the rather less idealistic viewpoint of the UK's national interests, although most would opine that integration

---

[14] Thatcher, p. 760. It is noteworthy that the different emphasis of the two nations chimes with their different political histories, particularly the youth of the German state and the background of its component states in the Holy Roman Empire with its Diet or Parliament.

[15] See Mody, A, *Greece and the Andre Szasz Axiom*, www.bruegel.org, sourced 24 February 2015.

[16] Tombs, Robert, *ed.,* Europeanism and Historical Myths in *European Demos, a historical myth?* London, 2014

has gone too far, the method Monnet has also produced UK supported free market reforms that would not otherwise have occurred.

The Treaty of Amsterdam to the Treaty of Lisbon

The themes outlined above leading to integration can be seen in the key treaty events since Maastricht summarised below.

The collapse of communism in Eastern Europe increased the number of candidate countries wishing to join the EU, but it was first Austria, Finland and Sweden that joined in 1995, Norway again failing to join after a referendum. This brought the EU membership to 15. With further enlargement on the cards further treaty reform was necessary. 1997 saw the Treaty of Amsterdam which saw the UK now led by Blair's Labour agreeing to the Social Chapter which became an official part of European law. The Schengen Agreement allowing travel without passport control among certain members was also incorporated into law. The Stability and Growth Pact, defining acceptable fiscal deficits and debt levels, was agreed for Eurozone candidates to ensure economic convergence, albeit it was subsequently broken by both Germany and France. The Treaty also required environmental protection requirements to be taken into account in all EU policies which proved to be the beginning of a subsequent major increase in the EU's emphasis on green issues.

In 1999, the entire commission led by Jacques Santer resigned following allegations of fraud, mismanagement and nepotism. Romani Prodi was appointed the new President of the Commission promising radical change with only a few of the old commissioners reappointed. This event still has influence today as the Commission, facing a more powerful Parliament is perceived to be more willing to lean towards the will of Parliament.

The Euro was introduced in 1999 when the initial member currency exchange rates were locked and in 2002 notes and coins began to circulate. A new focus on Europe's economic performance led to the negotiation of the "Lisbon Strategy" in 2000. This looked to encourage the structural reforms to improve Europe's growth and employment performance with a core role for the "knowledge economy" and to become "the most dynamic and socially inclusive economy in the world by 2010". With the benefit of hindsight if the necessary economic reforms had been undertaken, notably in Southern Europe, then the crisis in Southern Europe resulting from the euro crisis would have been ameliorated. Instead most feasted on the inflows of cheap and plentiful credit and avoided difficult reforms.

In 2000 the Charter of Fundamental Rights was proclaimed as a non binding legal declaration setting out 54 rights including the right to strike, marry, have a family, collective bargaining and fair working conditions. From that time the EU has looked to become more of a "rights" body that can claim increased legitimacy and favour among ordinary people.

In 2001 the Treaty of Nice introduced Qualified Majority Voting in 27 different areas. In 2004, one year after the treaty of Nice came into effect, the EU undertook its biggest enlargement with the accession of 10 members: Cyprus, Czech Republic, Estonia, Hungary, Latvia, Lithuania ,Malta, Poland, Slovakia and Slovenia increasing membership to twenty five and adding some hundred million to the population. Even critics of the EU view it as a great achievement for it have played a pivotal role in realigning the eastern bloc countries with the West. Aspiration to membership of the EU provided the motivation and justification for painful political and economic reforms through meeting the accession rules. Membership has also provided the relatively poor new entrants with substantial injections of new money and the security blanket of the EU and its integration aims. It has granted smaller countries the ability to participate in the governance of Europe, especially since the EU structure is designed to give them more weight. This was signified in December 2014 when the former Polish Prime Minister, Donald Tusk, became president of the European Council. Less positive for some nations has been the population migration from poor countries in substantial numbers and the sometimes resultant social implications. The Euro crisis has also demonstrated that smaller countries are forced to make adjustments that would seem inconceivable in France or Italy.

The enlargement together with the EU's expansion of activities brought to a head the need to undertake a fundamental reform of its working methods and decision processes. At the heart of the difficulties were the relative powers of Commission, Council and Parliament and the tension of pooling sovereignty versus national interests. Tony Blair, in particular, was keen to improve the effectiveness of the Council of Ministers to act as a counterbalance to the Commission and reflect national interests. He had found, in the words of his European advisor Roger Liddle, that it was attempting to handle "the challenges of twenty –first century interdependence with the toolkit of nineteenth century nation state diplomacy"[17]

The issues were discussed at the Convention on the Future of Europe which was chaired by the former French President, Giscard d'Estaing and met in 2002 -3. A draft Constitutional Treaty arose from an IGC in 2004 which proposed majority voting in the Council of Ministers for extended policy areas. A failure to justify it to national electorates, however, resulted in its rejection in referendums in France and the Netherlands, with the referendum causing major divisions among French socialists. The UK government was gratefully able to abandon its own plans for a referendum, but it is ironic that France only called theirs because of the popular pressure resulting from the original British decision.[18]With the UK referendum due to occur in 2017, the same year as the French Presidential elections, Hollande is motivated to avoid domestic pressures arising from a new British precedent.

Practical issues still had to be resolved and in 2007, the year Bulgaria and Romania entered the EU, bringing membership to 27, the Treaty of Lisbon was passed and included the necessary institutional reforms included in the rejected Constitution. This introduced QMV to more areas and created the new post of President of the European Council, replacing the rotating country presidency. The Charter of Fundamental rights became legally binding although several countries including the UK opted out, or at least thought they had. According to Giscard d'Estaing there were no significant differences to the original constitution, but while that process had attempted to be transparent and democratic the treaty process was undertaken by lawyers who made it "impenetrable to the public" and banished "Constitution" from the text.[19] Thus while the Constitution had been grandiose in its claims and had created a backlash, the Treaty included 90% of the Constitutions terms in a manner to avoid a referendum in most countries. The tortuous ratification process of the Lisbon Treaty has meant that many nations wish to avoid a future treaty, with implications for any UK renegotiations.

The EU's Foreign Policy Development

In the 1990's the EU failed to prevent or resolve the Bosnian and Kosovan wars and its policy response to the crises was viewed as an abject failure. Later efforts early in the Millennium to develop military capability primarily relied on the agreement of the UK and France as the key military powers, but were stifled by divisions on the intervention in Iraq.

[17] Liddle, Roger, *The* Europe *Dilemma*, London, 2014, p. 83
[18] Liddle, p. 136. Blair was forced to call a referendum after domestic political pressure which reportedly broke a prior deal with Chirac.
[19] d'Estaing, Giscard, "The EU Treaty is the same as the Constitution", in *The Independent,* 30 October 2007

The Lisbon Treaty included measures to bring more coherence to "common" foreign policy objectives by an enhanced role for the High Commissioner, (to be termed Foreign Minister until the UK objected), and the formation of a diplomatic corps, the European External Action Service. With the EU's competence over trade policy, its global leadership in Green policies and the foreign policy instruments of its aid budget and civilian crisis management capabilities, there was an opportunity for the EU to project more effectively its soft power and influence. To date, the outcome has been mixed with turf wars with the Commission over respective responsibilities and decisions driven inevitably by the lowest common denominator of member states. The European Parliaments attempts to link trade deals to human rights matters has also delayed some key trade agreements. There are differing ambitions for the reach of a "joint" EU foreign policy, with a recurrence of the pattern of some nation states resisting "power grabs" from an EU institution ambitious to increase its powers .In 2013 the High Representative, Baroness Ashton, did seal an initial peace agreement between Serbia and Kosovo and chaired the 6 power nuclear negotiations with Iran. But in 2011 the military intervention in Libya had split the EU with Germany leading opposition, reflecting its longstanding passive mind set.

The Ukrainian crisis, initially triggered in 2013 by progress towards an Association Agreement ("AA"), has illustrated themes of the EU's strengths and weaknesses in foreign policy which have been analysed by a House of Lords committee[20]. To be objective, the EU's lack of sensitivity to Russian concerns was a mistake shared by foreign policy at national level and in the US. It was part of a general western strategic failure to recognise changes in Russia and its attitude to the West over ten years, with the EU perceived as a stalking horse for NATO enlargement. Unfortunately, to the extent that Russia's hostility to the Ukrainian AA was latterly recognised, she was deemed too weak to prevent it and the EU indeed campaigned to accelerate the process. The EU basked in its prior successes in Eastern Europe and failed to recognise that for Russia it was not a strategic partner, but an opposing force. Even in direct trade negotiations with Russia, the EU viewed her as an aspiring member state in its "take it or leave it" approach. According to the Lords' Committee, all sides were surprised by the revolt in Ukrainian society when talks were suspended under Russian pressure, which confirmed the powerful attractions of the EU and its values to many nations located on its fringes. The EU had been largely operating in a political vacuum without national oversight and had failed to recognise the special status of Ukraine to Russia and the implications of its actions. Ukraine is now facing the disastrous consequences of the EU's naivety.

The Ukrainian crisis had required Germany to take a lead, due to close economic ties and the absence of US leadership, with ultimately a strong economic sanction response largely driven by Chancellor Merkel. However, the consensus driven process clearly has its limitations when facing an aggressive Putin and there has been no evidence that Germany, despite an internal debate, is willing to take a leadership role in foreign policy to reflect its economic power. The low defence budgets and weak hard power military capabilities of most member states, including Germany, is a clear weakness in the EU's ability to demonstrate leadership. Thus in 2014-5, in the crisis of Ukraine, the Ebola outbreak and ISIS there was no operational role for EU institutions.

The Euro crisis and its impact may be seen to reduce the EU's global influence and soft power in future years. With Russia working in a multitude of ways ranging from financial support to anti EU parties to gas supply tensions, the EU is facing an adversary it has underestimated and who is motivated to weaken or if possible tear up Europe's post- communist settlement. The key foreign policy challenge for the EU is its relationship with Russia. The fact that Commission President Juncker in March 2015 again raised the unrealistic objective of forming a European army, perhaps as

---

[20] House of Lords EU Committee, *The EU and Russia: before and beyond the crisis in Ukraine*, 23 March 2010.

an alternative to the rival power base of NATO, does not raise confidence that the EU is well prepared for future foreign policy challenges.

The Great Recession and the Euro Crisis

Soon after the Lisbon Treaty was passed and before it was even operational, the EU was plunged into crisis by the financial crisis which began in the US in 2008, but by 2009 was a sovereign debt crisis for some members for the Eurozone. Presented as the logical culmination of a single market, the euro from its adoption produced a convergence in interest rates and easy credit conditions, as it created a single euro capital market. The resultant boom in many Southern European markets and Ireland produced large (but not transparent) Euro balance of payments deficits in some countries and surpluses in others, notably Germany. German exporters were able to capitalise on demand with Spanish and other customers financed by German banks, while also benefiting from the fact that the euro provided Germany with an undervalued exchange rate. At the height of the bubble Spain was importing more capital than every other economy in the world other than the US, while Greece was the fifth largest importer.[21] The crisis from 2009 was focussed on the "PIIGS", which faced liquidity issues due to the inability of both their governments and financial institutions to raise debt. The halo of currency union and unified sovereign risk was shattered by the recognition that there were inadequate mechanisms to provide support, nor was there any consensus among euro countries that they should put rescue money at risk to support countries in difficulties.

The period since 2010 has seen a series of measures starting with the European Financial Stability Facility and culminating with the European Stability Mechanism in 2012 to enable debt restructuring and financial support and to police Eurozone budgets and deficits and impose sanctions for non compliance. The European institutions have struggled to react effectively due to differing national positions on burden sharing and the ECB's monetary policy response, particularly from Germany. The commitment of ECB President Draghi to do "whatever it takes " has been crucial in pulling the Euro back from the brink.

One casualty of the initial euro crisis was the ability of Italy to keep its own elected Prime Minister. Silvio Berlusconi was effectively pushed out in late 2011 to increase Italian economic credibility and subsequent Prime Ministers have not been democratically elected. Despite this EU intervention in the Italian democratic process, the continued failure of Italy to reform has meant that debt to GDP has continued to rise as the economy has stalled. In 2014 public debt was close to 137%, the third highest in the world after Japan and Greece. Another casualty has been Cyprus, where the 2013 banking crisis led to private depositors taking a haircut in the restructuring of the banking sector when the banks were closed for 7 days. To this day who took the decisions in the EU institutions which led to major economic disruption in an EU state is opaque. In due course Cyprus has obtained a €2.5bn loan from Russia with whom it already had close economic ties and in early 2015 it was announced that the Russian navy would be allowed to use Cypriot port facilities despite the UK bases on the island. The evolving crisis in Greece, where GDP has fallen by 25% and debt is unsustainably high, may ultimately lead to their withdrawal from the euro and a crisis for other

---

[21] Klein, Matthew, *Michael Pettis explains the Euro crisis*,www.ftalphaville.ft.com, sourced on 6 February 2015. Pettis also makes the historic comparison that Germany's economy suffered greatly from the bubble from large capital inflows resulting from French reparations in 1871-3 as with Spain in the Euro era. So much for "national character". There is also the interesting cultural differentiation about who is to blame for the Euro crisis, the creditor or the debtor and the philosophically different positions concerning debt forgiveness between, for example, Germany and the US.

vulnerable nations. With the benefit of hindsight, it is now clear that the economic conditions imposed by the EU and the IMF for the initial Greek bailouts were not correct and were primarily designed to protect the euro from breakup, rather than assist Greece.

The EU has thus not protected smaller countries from economic storms, indeed they have all endured challenging economic adjustments, while at the same time France has sought and obtained relief from its own deficit reduction targets. This repeats the 2003 experience when France and Germany combined to stop fines being imposed by the EU for breaking the 3% deficit limits. There are reports that Germany wishes to put decisions on deficit rules in a new institution away from the more malleable Commission. Most importantly, the rules focus on deficits rather than ensuring macro economic balance. For over 5 years Germany has run a current account surplus in excess of 6 % of GDP and is forecast to reach a high of 7.9% in 2015.[22] It is technically subject to fines, but they are not enforced by the Commission and will lead to further major imbalances within the Eurozone.

One factor that demonstrates the divisions in the Eurozone is the fact that German economic thinking and its political class utilise an economic model, ordoliberalism, not shared with any other nation and resulting from its economic experience in the inter war years. This is based on the principle that rules are imposed by the government to ensure markets are not captured by vested interests or cartels.[23] The role of the State (which is itself faces its own rules to keep it honest), is to monitor compliance, but everyone is liable for their own actions. In the words of Jurgen Stark, former ECB board member "From this perspective the most important principles are the primacy of price stability; the promotion of competition in all markets; the protection of property rights; freedom of contract; and the idea that individuals should bear the risks of their own decisions and the losses of banks should not be borne by the whole of society."[24] Probably a philosophy not too far away from Eurosceptic centre right politicians in the UK, but a country mile away from the political culture in much of France and Southern Europe.

This is how Germany expected the Euro to operate, with nations sorting out their own competitiveness issues by internal reform, rather like the interwar gold standard but without the option of abandoning the peg. However, other nations have not had that discipline even with German concessions.[25] In the words of former US Treasury Secretary Geithner, it made Berlin "just paranoid that every act of generosity was met by sort of a f**k you from the (political) establishment of the weaker countries in Europe".[26] It has also driven the German target of a balanced budget and a perplexing belief that all members of the Eurozone can and should run a current account surplus. Germany and its people never wanted to adopt the Euro and the implications of fiscal and banking union. Each policy action to the crisis which has meant more exposure to weak Euro nations has been resisted by Germany. In the end Germany will have to either accept the implications of the euro or lead the adoption of new arrangements, which could include a German led northern European core exiting the euro area.

---

[22] Evans-Pritchard, Ambrose, "Germany's record trade surplus is a bigger threat to the euro than Greece", in *The Daily Telegraph*, 5 May 2015.

[23] Munchau, Wolfgang, "The wacky economics of Germanys parallel universe", in the *Financial Times*, 16 November 2014

[24] Stark, Jurgen, "The historical and cultural differences that divide Europe's Union", in the *Financial Times*, 12 February 2015

[25] A favourite analogy is how the individual US state indebtedness are their own obligations and thus they learnt through history, particularly after the 1836 crisis, to live within their means or default. It ignores the much larger federal fiscal transfers than in the EU and ironically the resistance to writing off Greek debt.

[26] Aldrick, Philip, "Germany seems to have forgotten that rules are made to be broken", in *The Times* , 29 November 2014

The Condition of the EU in 2015

The Euro should probably have been the last stage of integration in the development of an "optimal currency area", but for the political objectives of Europe, an enormous monetary experiment was undertaken far too soon and with implications that are still to be fully seen. In particular, the poor economic performance of the Eurozone and the high levels of unemployment and uncompetitiveness of Southern European economies creates issues that are impossible to resolve without further economic and political integration or exits from the Eurozone. In the meantime the rise of anti austerity parties is raising tensions in many member states.

The EU's leaders and supporters traditionally boast about the EU's important role in European peace and prosperity. However recent events make this increasingly easy to question. For different reasons the EU is in danger of creating two failed states in Greece and the Ukraine. The 2014 European Parliament elections not only saw a low turnout, but also the rise in the representation of protest parties from both the right and the left, that was seen in the EU institutions as major blow to the EU's philosophy. There is now much concern as to the outcome of the 2019 parliamentary elections and a new humility and recognition that the EU is in crisis and must change. In the early 1980's a lesser economic crisis led to the impetus for the Single European Act. In 2015 there is another opportunity which could again lead to reforms in the UK's interests.

THE INSTITUTIONS OF THE EU

The Facts. The EU states share sovereignty in a range of policy areas and make decisions on laws proposed by the European Commission which are debated in the Council of Ministers and European Parliament which make decisions on a co-decision basis. This now covers most policy areas including justice and "home affairs" such as combating discrimination and consumer affairs. In the Council a veto is retained over social security, tax and defence matters, but otherwise Qualified Majority Voting (QMV) based on population size and a 65% vote is utilised.

The UK parliament must implement EU law and obey rulings of the European Court of Justice (ECJ). There are three types of legislation. Regulations are directly applicable in member states (eg common rules on aircraft passenger compensation). Directives, which set out the aims members have to adhere to, but rely on nations to introduce in the manner they wish to. Finally, Decisions are directly binding on nation states or individuals.

The EU can only act within its areas of competence which are set out in the Treaties. EU competence can be exclusive, shared with a nation or run parallel with a nation. With a shared competence, once the EU exercises its competence, the nation may no longer share, unless the EU withdraws by repealing legislation. Acquis, also known as the "acquis communautaire" is the combined laws of the EU comprised of Treaties, Regulations, Directives, Decisions, supplementary or enabling Delegated Acts and Implementing Acts, and the case law of the ECJ. The ECJ has provided some 28000 judgments. It works solely in French with its plaintiffs being not citizens but governments, EU institutions and businesses. However a private citizen may appear before it if an EU decision is of "direct concern" to them personally.

An understanding of the process of integration, the culture of the EU and the resultant issues the UK has faced, requires us to understand how the institutions developed and operate in response to the Treaties. It particularly reflects the EU's constantly expansionary ambition at the expense of the nation state and the power of its rule based authority.

The Commission, the Council of Ministers and Parliament

The history of the EU has shown that the Commission and its President have been key drivers of development. It is a political body that initiates legislation combined with the administrative function of a civil service. With one Commissioner appointed by each member state, it has a quasi-judicial authority to police markets and ensure compliance with regulations. The Council of Ministers is the vehicle where governments meet to agree policies, coordinate national policies and resolve differences between themselves and other EU institutions. It is thus also part of the executive, but also performs a legislative role with the European Parliament, as after the Commission has put forward a new law or policy, the two bodies discuss and amend the proposals and each must then approve them, ("the co –decision process").

The European Parliament is the EU institution that has changed the most in the process of integration and become much more powerful. It is Parliament that is able to remove the Commission, as it illustrated in 1999 by forcing the resignation of the Santer Commission. In 2014 Parliament introduced, via the terms of the Treaty of Lisbon, the "spitzenkandidaten "process where each leading parliamentary group nominated a candidate for presidency of the Commission. The centre right EPP grouping won the most votes in the 2014 elections and then claimed that their candidate, Jean- Claude Juncker had won a "popular mandate" and thus national governments were obliged to nominate him. This was despite his lack of recognition to the European electorate or any general understanding that they were voting for a candidate. There was some ambiguity on the legal legitimacy of Parliament's claim, however, in the event, the European Council of national leaders did recommend Junker on a QMV. The eventual support of Chancellor Merkel was seen as conclusive and confirmed again the German elites belief in power being exercised by the Parliament. This is helpfully supported by the main German political parties both having very strong influence in the main European groupings to ensure German interests are well protected.[27]

Only the UK and Hungary voted against spitzenkandidaten, the UK due to Junker's federalist leanings and the dangers of the precedent of granting even more powers to the Parliament and politicising the role of the Commission President, by his election by a parliamentary group. This parliamentary assertiveness was subsequently demonstrated in the hearing of potential commissioners (one of whom was rejected), where MEP's attempted to influence commissioners on their objectives in their roles and potentially rejecting those with the "wrong views".[28] The dysfunctionality of the process was indicated by the fact that commissioner candidates were politicians, but were expected in hearings to have technocratic knowledge on a brief they had in most cases never overseen. Moreover MEP's selection criteria was inconsistent ranging across political allegiance, expertise and nationality.

This now strong influence over the Commission by Parliament is often not viewed positively by national officials and is said to be producing "legal activism" by the Commission, prodded by Parliament. The UK Europe Minister, David Lidington, in his oral evidence to the European Select Committee, remarked that "the centre of gravity of Parliament was to regard greater European integration "as a self evident good" and the overall working culture of the Commission and Parliament was to prefer integration. The Commission, "looking over its shoulder at the Santer Commission" has been "ever more willing to lean towards the Parliament and adjust its proposals and approach to negotiations to try and make sure it gets the agreement of Parliament. In my view, this has been done at the expense of the views of national governments represented in the Council. There has been an institutional shift". According to Lidington this institutional shift was a recent development.[29]

The democratic legitimacy of Parliament for this increased power is questionable. The two main centre left and centre right MEP groupings voted the same way 74% of the time in 2009-14, increasing to 80 % since June 2014, which suggests that they are more interested in increasing their own powers than representing their electorates. With the centralist Liberals also normally voting in the same manner, approximately two thirds of MEP's appear aligned with supporting the EU "establishment", versus its critics from a variety of backgrounds.[30] Moreover, over the past 20 years turnout in European elections has fallen from 57% to *43%.*[31]The strategy of increasing MEP's democratic legitimacy by systematically increasing their powers has thus not been effective, but this has not discouraged Parliament from promoting the extension of European wide "rights " for its citizens as an attempted route to increasing its popularity.

---

[27] Confirmed in a conversation with Christopher Howarth, Senior Policy Analyst at Open Europe on 20 March 2015. A less idealistic explanation for Merkel's support arises from powerful German media support for Juncker due to his promise to challenge Google's dominance.

[28] Open Europe, www.openeurope.org, sourced 3 October 2014.

[29] Questions to D Lidington by House of Commons Select Committee on European Scrutiny 4 July 2013.

[30] Barber, Tony, "EU Parliament's major parties vote together", in the *Financial Times*, 11 March 2015

[31] Booth, Stephen & Howarth, Chrisopher, *The European Parliament: A failed experiment in pan European democracy?* London, 2014

Decision Making in Practice

Other than highly political matters most decisions are the result of a three way dynamic known as the trilogue between Commission officials, MEP's with a specialism in a particular area and national civil servants supported by their Brussels based Permanent Representatives. However, it is prior to the trilogue that a clear direction is set with lobbyists and special interests playing an important role. Corporate Europe Observatory report that there are at least 30,000 lobbyists in Brussels.[32] Sir John Cunliffe, former UK Permanent Representative confirmed, "everyone knows, much of Europe is about influencing early on in the process rather than at the trilogue stage". [33]Even then, in the words of First Vice President Frans Timmermans, "It is hard for people not directly involved in them to know either when they (the trilogue) would take place or what was agreed".[34]

According to Roger Liddle while the trilogue is full of institutional tensions, it also forms an "incestuous partnership". Commission officials are often technically more competent than British civil servants as they move jobs less frequently, senior MEP's specialise in particular committee work and the parliamentary committees generally work to achieve cross party consensus between the key parliamentary groups. National civil servants also have wide discretion as long as they avoid political controversy.[35] In the words of Liddle, "The Commission and Parliament are the most visible Brussels player; yet national civil servants also exert huge influence...Officials have a wide discretion as long as they avoid political controversy. There is a built in preference for opacity; as a technique for getting agreement it usually works. The Brussels system provides national officials with an opportunity to achieve reforms through the EU that can be more difficult to achieve domestically.....objections from other departments would have to be overcome.... consensus with (Brussels) colleagues can be easier to achieve because of shared institutional and specialist interests"[36]. It is indeed the case that much of the decision making takes place below Council/Ministerial level. "Coreper" the committee of national permanent representatives is in a "pivotal" position in the decision making process with many of its agreements not voted on by ministers.[37] This important role for the Coreper process which has increased centralisation in the EU decision making process, has made it more difficult for individual government departments to influence the decisions reached.

The lack of public accountability is reinforced further by the fact that although a vote is taken in Parliament, unlike in Westminster, legislation can be passed on a First reading. From 2009-14, 85% of legislation was passed at the First Reading stage making it very challenging for any national parliament to scrutinise proposals properly, especially as new compromises can appear late in the day often through " informal trilogues" with individual nations unrepresented. In the words of the European Scrutiny Committee, "The unpredictable nature of First Reading deals and trilogue negotiations can render scrutiny at national level difficult if not impossible".[38] The UK Government may well see advantages in the weakness of effective scrutiny by Westminster, but combined with

---

[32] Traynor, Ian, "30,000 lobbyists and counting", in *The Guardian* 8 May 2014
[33] Oral evidence to Commons Select Committee on European Scrutiny quoted in Twenty-Fourth Report of 2013-14, 20 November 2013, p. 24
[34] Timmermans, Frans, in *EU observer blog,*https://euobserver.com, sourced 3 February 2015
[35] Liddle, p. 107
[36] Liddle, p. 107-8
[37] House of Commons European Scrutiny report, *Reforming the European scrutiny system in the House of Commons*, 20 November 2013, p. 29
[38] House of Commons European Scrutiny Committee report, *Reforming the European scrutiny system in the House of Commons*, p. 25.

the compromises of QMV, the likelihood of legislation being passed not in the UK's national interests or with unintended consequences is high. Thus in 2013 a late amendment to legislation on bank capital adequacy by the European Parliament led to an EU cap on bankers bonuses being introduced and the UK being outvoted on a financial services policy for the first time. UK influence has also likely to have reduced further by the 2014 elections, which made UKIP the largest grouping with 24 of the 73 seats, given their general disinterest in the legislative process.

The consequences of the Brussels Decision Making Process

The Centre for European Reform and Open Europe are two respected think tanks that are among many that hold the view that the EU has grown to a size incompatible with its institutions and objectives. The CBI, also perceived as pro Europe has also offered criticisms of the EU's institutions. Key points the three bodies raise include:[39]

- Because of the complexity of the decision making it is not always evident who is responsible for taking decisions and how they can be held to account. Once regulations are in place they are very difficult to change.
- Insufficient respect by the Commission of the will of national parliaments, insufficient attention to proportionality and subsidiarity.
- Adding functions and "mission creep".
- Lobby groups and special interests, some of them financed by the EU, are able to exert significant and on occasions excessive influence including an important role in impact assessments.
- There are not enough jobs for the 28 Commissioners to do and their objectives may conflict. Moreover, perhaps due to circumstances, the Commission President has been perceived as ineffective in leading and coordinating.
- Insufficient attention to subsidiarity and too many or too detailed rules. For example in 2013 the Commission proposed, banning restaurants serving olive oil in reusable bottles, introducing quotas for women on corporate boards and outlawing menthol cigarettes. Only the later was adopted, but all were not consistent with subsidiarity and reflected the Commission's constant impulse to legislate.
- Unsatisfactory impact assessments of regulations and not enough attention on the impact on SME's and micro businesses.
- Legal activism by Parliament, both in promoting legislation not popular with nation states (eg 2013 proposals for 20 weeks maternity leave). Parliament is also able to link matters such as monitoring human rights to free trade agreements in negotiation, which is delaying agreements. It is perhaps inevitable that MEP's want to do more, rather than less, but it again works against subsidiarity. In the US over the past 10-15 years, many aspects of welfare policy have been downstreamed to the state level, but the European parliament has the opposite intended direction of travel.
- A bloated expensive bureaucracy with high pay and a "jobs for life culture". Speaking of the Commission retiring in 2014 one commentator reported "The European Commission has evolved into dens of intrigue and bitter personality clashes. Above all, it has become an institution where individuals are not encouraged to speak up about its weaknesses or the incompetence of senior, tenured, and very well paid staff."[40] The UK's own civil service and

---

[39] See Grant, Charles, *How to build a modern European Union,* London, 2015
   Open Europe, *An eleven point mandate for the next European Commission,* Briefing Paper, 8 September 2014.

[40] Dempsey, Judy, *Carnegie Europe,* www.carnegieeurope.eu, sourced 10 September 2014

most other government administrations do of course share the characteristics of being to some extert self serving and resistant to change. What is perhaps different in the EU bureaucracy is that its leading officials transparently promote the political objectives and ideals of closer and closer integration.

- A budget and spending pattern that is widely acknowledged as neither efficient or necessarily channelling funds to the most productive area. The EU budget in 2014 of €142bn was only about 2% of total government expenditure of member states, but with 40% of that sum spent on farmer and countryside support, substituting entirely for member state spending in that field.[41] A further 34% is allocated to the structural fund to promote economic growth, but a third of that is allocated to poor regions in rich countries and involves an inefficient channelling to and then back from Brussels. Moreover, national and regional governments must source eligible projects to use the pre a located funding budget, which puts an emphasis on ensuring funds are fully used rather than necessarily well spent. This criticism is supported by the EU budgetary committee that reported a 2014 "error rate" of 5.2% for funds spent by countries against 3.7 % by the Commission. In either case it was above the auditor's standard of 2% leading to the continued pattern of qualification of the EU's accounts.[42] Critics say that spending allocation to cross border energy transmission or transport projects would be a better use for funds and a November 2014 initiative to seed growth building infrastructure investment of a planned E350bn was criticised by its restriction to E20bn due to the EU's lack of firepower.

The new Commission led by Juncker seems to be taking many of the governance criticisms seriously. In an important innovation Commissioners are for the first time grouped under Senior Vice Presidents which co ordinate policy in related areas and are working on the mantra that the Commission should be "big on the big things and small on the small things". A First Vice President, Frans Timmermans, with a strong reforming track record in the Commission has been tasked with cutting EU red tape and emphasising subsidiarity. He is reported as saying that it is the most difficult job he has ever had and that "first of all we need to change the attitude that only if I make a law am I contributing...we believe we don't exist if we don't make laws"[43] Certainly there is an acceptance in the Commission that the EU is facing a crisis which it is attempting to respond to and the Commission annua paper on its business for 2015 saw a reduction in initiat ves from the usual average of around 100 to 23. In the words of Kay Swinburne MEP "reform is top of everyone's agenda in Europe ".[44]

The Implementation of Brussels Decisions: European Law and the European Court of Justice

Critics often complain about the massive European bureaucracy, but it is actually small. With about 31,000 staff it is less than that of Birmingham City Council. It relies on laws and the courts and the litigation of interested private actors to enforce the resultant *acquis communautaire*. The European Court of Justice (ECJ) has been at the forefront of the process of deepening integration by interpreting and expanding the reach of European law. Founded in 1952 initially to support the ECSC, it arose from the requirement to interpret Treaty terms and settle challenges and disputes at a level above the nation state.

---

[41] Europa.eu website. www.europa-eu, statistics on EU budget sourced 6 November 2014

[42] Open Europe, statistics on error rate in EU spending http://openeurope.org.uk/daily-shakeup/eurozone-officials-dash-greek-hopes-of-securing-e1-2bn-from-bailout-fund/,sourced 26 March 2015

[43] Timmermans, Frans, quoted in Euobserver blog, https://euobserver.com, sourced 3 February 2015

[44] Speaking at a City of London/Open Europe Conference on 20 January 2015

As the treaties have expanded the scope of Europe, the Court's rulings have had greater impact. The European Single Market Act was the greatest spur to heightened activity and most recently the Treaty of Lisbon has further increased its reach to cover all activities of the EU except for common foreign and security policy, with the Charter of Fundamental Rights legal adoption beginning to cause ripples and controversy. The ECJ's new interactions, of course, complements the increased activism of Parliament. The Maastricht Treaty had introduced the principle of Subsidiarity to EU action. Under this principle, outside areas of exclusive EU competence, "The Union shall act only if and insofar as the objectives of the proposed action cannot be sufficiently achieved by the Member state at national regional or local level "[45] However, the "ever closer union" spirit of the original Treaty of Rome and the ambitions of the ECJ and others has meant it has had little impact. The ECJ has been able to take the view that almost all proposals for EU wide action can be best achieved at EU level.

The progression into the field of human rights can perhaps be viewed as a means of obtaining legitimacy for the ECJ and the democratic role of the European Parliament via "popular legalism ".[46] What is evident is that through judicial power and more regulation enforced through litigation, we are now closer to the US model of "adversarial legalism". Transparent legally enforceable rules which can be framed as "rights" that can be pursued legally by third parties has been the mechanism for pushing integration.[47]

The powerful combination of the "Direct Effect "and Preliminary Rulings.

Early on, the ECJ established the "primacy" of EU law and the ECJ over national courts and the concept of "direct effect". This was firstly in 1963 through the case of Van Gen den Loos, which involved a customs duty dispute on the import of good from Germany to the Netherlands, the ECJ argued that the Treaty of Rome created a supranational constitution which, unlike conventional treaties between nations, could be applied in national courts beneath it. As Luuk Van Middelaar, adviser to president of the European Council explains:

"Lawyers discern in it the birth of..."direct effect"-the principle that individuals can, in certain circumstances, appeal to the treaty over the heads of the states...Every national judge was henceforth a European judge. He or she had a duty to apply European regulations, not through the ECJ but within any court of justice...From this point on any participant in economic life-manufacturer, wholesaler, employee, consumer-could force a member state to adhere to these rules"[48]

A year later in Costa v ENEL the judges went a stage further and ruled that the Treaty of Rome was supreme over national law and thus the national courts were subservient to the ECJ in the areas covered by the Treaty. This claim of legal supremacy would become more and more significant as the scope of the EU expanded. What it meant radically was that the "judges had decided that the real guardians of the Treaty would be citizens and firms seeking their rights before the courts...over the heads of the national decision makers"[49] As with the development of the formal institutions it was the assertive idealism of officials, in this case judges, which led to the early rulings and contributed to the supranational agenda. From these key judgements onwards, the next 20 or so years saw a battle between an activist court and its supporters, who sought out test cases suitable

---

[45] Article 5(3) of the Treaty on the European Union.

[46] Kelemen, R. Daniel, *Rorotoko,* www.rorotoko.com, 19 September 2011, sourced 10 August 2015.

[47] Kelemen, *Rorotoko,* sourced 10 August 2015.

[48] Brady, Hugo, *12 things everyone should know about the European Court of Justice,* London, 2014, p.16.

[49] Brady, p. 17

for referral to the ECJ, and nation states, some of who (such as France), ignored some rulings, just as they would other international courts. As the breadth of the EU has increased the potential for conflict with national constitutional courts has widened.

The key mechanism for the expansion of the role of the ECJ has been the preliminary ruling procedure, which was utilised in both the key cases above. This is the process where a national court refers a case to the ECJ to obtain an interpretation of EU law. The rulings are based on the specifics of the case and thus do not often give much discretion to decide a case differently from the ruling. Thus national courts can work with the ECJ to make law, even perhaps in conflict with the wishes of a national government or even a higher national court. From the ECJ viewpoint it enables the uniformity of decisions among nation states and developed and clarified law, but it has also led to conflicts with national governments, national supreme courts and constitutions. To bolster its position in 1990 the case of Francovich and Others established that a state could be held liable for its failure to fulfil treaty obligations[50], while also in 1990 the case of Factorame established that courts must issue injunctions to prevent governments taking action that is contrary to EU law. Fines can be imposed by the European Commission for breaches of European Law.

Human Rights

According to Hugo Brady by the time of the 2004 enlargement the Court had helped remove most fundamental legal obstacles to the single market and from then on rulings focussed more on social policy, labour relations, consumer protection and the environment.[51] The legal status given to the Charter of Fundamental Rights by the Lisbon Treaty has enabled new actors, such as human rights activists to utilise the Court and test national or even EU rulings against the Charter. The strategy used by human rights NGO's is to select the best national jurisdiction to maximise the chance of an application for a ECJ preliminary ruling. Thus, in 2011, the Test-Achlat's case struck down the EU's efforts to exempt the insurance industry from its equal rights laws and resulted in the outlawing of gender based lower car insurance charges. Another example is, via an application from the Irish courts in 2014, the ECJ annulled the EU's data retention directive (which had required telecoms companies to keep personal telephone and internet records), on the basis that it breached the privacy rights of Europeans. Thus while the ECJ has greatly assisted the growth in EU power the application of the Charter may ultimately constrain its powers and for some this was an important factor in giving it legal status.[52] Another motivator has been the concern that some former communist members are sliding backwards into authoritarianism and heavy corruption. The pan European law and justice aspirations of the EU are partially driven by the wish to counter the backsliding occurring once accession rules have been met and to deepen the impact of liberal European attitudes. For example in 2015 the Commission has launched infringement proceedings against the Czech government relating to discrimination against Roma peoples.

---

[50] In this case the Italian state was held negligent by not implementing rules to protect employees owed wages from their company becoming insolvent.
[51] Brady, p. 22
[52] Lord Goldsmith's evidence, *House of Commons European Scrutiny Committee forty third report*, 26 March 2014, Section 2, p. 15.

A UK perspective on the reach of EU law

As noted above there are tensions between the ECJ and national supreme courts. However while, for example Germany can look for protections from its own written constitution ("Basic Laws"), the UK, with no constitution to invoke has no such protection, other than taking a decision it disagrees with to the ECJ. Indeed the 1972 European Communities Act 1972 means, according to Supreme Court judge Lord Mance, that there are few limits to the dominance of EU law. Quoted in a 2014 select committee report, he has said that through the Act all obligations arising under European treaties:

"are without further enactment to be given legal effect or be used in the UK. This gives rise to a paradox. Having so stipulated, no explicit constitutional buttress remains against incursion by EU law whatever. Indeed, the 1972 Act has itself been given a constitutional status lifting it above ordinary statutes"[53]

The loss of sovereignty due to the Act was first raised by Enoch Powell at the time it went on the statute books. It is, at best, unclear if the UK Supreme Court can invoke its powers to interpret the UK's "unwritten constitution "against EU laws and their interpretation by the ECJ. This issue has received judicial attention recently given the interpretation that the UK did not successfully opt out of the Charter of Fundamental Rights and its application by the ECJ in its rulings. The likelihood is that the Charter will be used in the UK courts for rights-based claims, which has resulted in a select committee recommendation that primary legislation should be passed to amend the 1972 act to exclude the Charter from its terms.[54] Perhaps the 2015 Conservative administration's intention to introduce a UK Bill of Rights will address this question, which is part of the wider issue of the division of power between Parliament and the judiciary.

Policing and criminal justice is another area where EU involvement has been controversial, despite a general acceptance that the police in Europe must work together. The Lisbon Treaty introduced Europe wide legislation which the UK mainly opted out of with a time limit for a final decision. In December 2014 the UK agreed to remain in the Europe Arrest warrant scheme. Providing another example of the trade off's of the EU , the benefits of speedy extradition of a terrorist from Italy to the UK, had to be set against extradition of UK citizens without possibility for appeal to jurisdictions with different legal cultures, which has resulted in some injustices.

Reflections on the workings of European Institutions and European Law from a UK perspective.

This paper has examined the workings of the trilogue decision making process and its implementation through the ECJ. It seems to work effectively for the machine, but lacks democratic accountability. In the words of Hugo Brady "it reflects the tendency to move difficult conflicts away from politicians to "apolitical groups of national experts, the legal realm and the courts"[55] Delors boasted unwisely in 1988 that 80 % of legislation would originate from Brussels within 10 years. There has been no definitive figure available, however, including statutory instruments, Business for Britain has calculated that 66.7% can be deemed to be influenced by either EU regulations (59.3%) or EU Directives (5.4%)[56] .The principle of subsidiarity has been ignored[57]. It has meant that the

---

[53] House of Commons European Scrutiny Committee, *The Application of the EU Charter of Fundamental Rights in the UK: a state of confusion,* 26 March 2014 para. 137.
[54] House of Commons European Scrutiny Committee, para. 172
[55] Brady, p. 23.
[56] See Philpott, Tim, *7% or 75%. The EU's influence over British Law: The definitive answer,* London, 2015
[57] Of course, it depends how you define subsidiarity. As previously noted the ECJ has taken the view that as the

direction of travel is that which is in the interests of the institutional machine. This usually means more integration, more power for itself and measures that demonstrate its own importance above that of the nation state. The EU's emphasis on regional initiatives and financial support within nation states is also helpful to this process.

The following comment on the internal workings of the UK government from Dominic Cummings, former special advisor to Michael Gove at the Department of Education, provides a poignant viewpoint :

"One of the things that is most striking is how much of a Cabinet Minister's box is filled with EU papers….. In order to continue the pretence that Cabinet Government exists, all these EU papers are circulated in the red boxes. Nominally, these are 'for approval'. They have a little form attached for the Secretary of State to tick. *However, because they are EU papers, this 'approval' process is pure Potemkin village.* If a Cabinet Minister replies saying – 'I do not approve, this EU rule is stupid and will cost a fortune' – then someone from the Cabinet Office calls their Private Office and says, 'Did your Minister get pissed last night, he appears to have withheld approval on this EU regulation.' If the Private Office replies saying 'No, the minister actually thinks this is barmy and he is withholding consent', then Llewellyn [PM's Chief of Staff] calls them to say 'ahem, old boy, the PM would prefer it if you lie doggo on this one'. In the very rare cases where a Minister is so infuriated that he ignores Llewellyn, then Heywood [Cabinet Secretary] calls to explain to them that they have no choice but to approve, so please tick your box and send in your form, pronto. Game over.

It is the sort of thing you read in history books about how a capital city operated just before the regime collapsed. Like many aspects of contemporary Whitehall, if one put it in a satire, nobody would believe it. It also shows how persistent the *'form'* of constitutions can be long after the *'reality'* has changed. It seemed to me a bad tactic for officials to do this as it is a weekly reminder of the ministers' impotence / irrelevance, and if I were a standard official in Cabinet Office I would probably knock it on the head – out of sight, out of mind. But as I type these words another thought occurs – perhaps they are behaviourists and they think that if they get the Cabinet into the mindset of just ticking things without reading them, then Whitehall's interests are well served. Maybe that explains why so few ministers ever complain about it. However, I think that it has also polarised people. A few will be confirmed in their view that 'there is no alternative to the EU, keep the mechanisms hidden' but there are certainly others who increasingly think 'this is a joke, we can't go on like this'."[58]

Dominic Cummings views resonate with Roger Liddle's earlier comment on the attractiveness of the EU model to UK civil servants, after all it is a good excuse for blocking political initiatives, and with David Lidington's comments on all EU institutions (including the main political groupings in the European Parliament), regarding greater integration as a self evident good. According to David Frost, this should not be interpreted as meaning that UK civil servants are all Europhiles, but it does reflect the fact that the civil service culture is to compromise in decision making within the rules of engagement, rather than create controversy by challenging the European status quo. Officials (and probably many ministers) are looking to solve a problem rather than create one and with QMV they will undoubtedly be driven by the centre of gravity. For the UK renegotiation this indicates the importance of the ground work to develop what is acceptable in the European political culture. In the case of immigration, for example, Frost believes the UK narrative over an extended period has moved the debate onto "normal" territory that would not have been acceptable in 2010.[59]

objective is uniformity the EU is normally the correct level for decision making.
[58] Cummings, Dominic, *Statement on the Working of Government*, www.dominiccummings.wordpress.com, sourced 7 August 2014.
[59] Frost, David, *Gearing up for delivery: How to manage the negotiation*, Open Europe, London, 2015 and discussion at Open Europe conference on 16 February 2015.

What if the UK was to decide to leave? ("Brexit")

The only established legal route to leave the EU is Article 50. Once triggered there is no turning back and the UK would be excluded from EU decisions on the new arrangements for the UK. Thus it would likely to be the final stage after arrangements have been negotiated. According to Open Europe, Brexit would require a consent chain to include a QMV of the Council, national Parliaments for some aspects and the unpredictable European Parliament. In the case of the latter it is possible that a French led protectionist bloc could command a blocking minority of 35% and influence the trading terms offered to the UK.[60] In addition, FTA's negotiated by the EU would also not automatically apply to the UK and may require negotiations with the fifty five countries and territories where the EU has preferential trading arrangements. These could probably be easily negotiated on current terms, but better arrangements for the UK could be subject to much longer timescales. Other issues requiring negotiation would include the status of EU nationals in the UK and vice versa, while the UK Parliament would have to go through a long process of reviewing UK law as EU law would have to remain in place initially including a wide pool which relies on reference to UK law.

The conclusion is that Brexit would be a very difficult process creating much uncertainty. Given that it would also be viewed as a negative outcome for the remaining EU to loose one of its largest members and biggest budget contributors, the UK could not presume that Brexit negotiations would be concluded in an atmosphere of helpful cordiality.

In conclusion, our review of the EU's development and the operation of its institutions has confirmed the integrationist motivations of the key actors and the substantial loss of sovereignty to the UK. In an interdependent world and given the UK's relative size it can be argued that the UK should face up to reality as to her individual impotence and that the EU is providing the UK with a true influence over her destiny. The UK should focus on maximising its influence in the EU given the complexities of Brexit. We will examine in the next section if this has been reflected in the UK's attitude to the EU.

---

[60] See Booth Stephen, et al, *What if? The consequences, challenges and opportunities facing Britain outside the EU,* Open Europe, London, 2015

THE UNITED KINGDOM'S ATTITUDE TO THE EU THROUGH ITS HISTORY

"Is Europe a prison or a castle?". This was a question posed at a London conference in the autumn of 2014[61]. As the delegates were discussing the EU's attack on the "Anglo Saxon" economic model of the City of London, the views of the participants were unequivocally, a prison. The puzzle is, that the "City" has largely been a traditional supporter of the EU and indeed of the Euro when it was introduced, but is now with government assistance attempting to fight off what many view as attacks from the EU to diminish it. In the general British populace, enthusiasm for the EU remains very weak with Eurobarometer attitude surveys showing a consistently negative attitude. Moreover, only a third of the UK sample identified themselves even on a secondary basis as "European", compared with the mean average of all other EU states of 59 %.[62] The UK had the lowest ranking by far of any country. This is not a new development, large sections of the public, and indeed many politicians, have always viewed " Europe " as some Continental "other" and this has been reflected in the press and political discourse throughout the UK's engagement.

Early Years

Winston Churchill was famously a strong supporter of the European ideal. Speaking in Zurich on 19th September 1947, he said:

"If Europe were once united in the sharing of its common inheritance, there would be no limit to the happiness, to the prosperity and glory which its three or four hundred million people would enjoy…….We must build a United States of Europe….The first step in the recreation of the European family must be a partnership between France and Germany."

However this enthusiasm did not extend to it being accepted by the immediate post war governments as something the UK should participate in. Although exhausted and with major economic problems, UK foreign policy reflected her world power and war victor status, however tenuous that strength might have been. There was "no overriding priority" among the three circles of influence that Britain held, consisting of the USA, the Empire/Commonweath and Europe[63]. The supranationalism required of European membership was seen to diminish the UK's influence with the USA and the Commonwealth. This was a cross party consensus and joining the ECSC was not seen in either our foreign or economic interests[64], nor was it thought to be likely to succeed. Economically the UK's strong trade ties with the old empire also meant there was little economic incentive seen to join when the EEC emerged. This meant that the unique institutional configuration and culture of the EEC was formed without the UK's influence . The future was to demonstrate that this was a crucial strategic error.

The UK's failure to engage seriously at this early stage was the first example of unexpected consequences arising from the UK's policy towards the Community. Once the UK joined, political parties have fluctuated in their views because of the ideological conflicts Europe produces. Perhaps the only powerful actor that since the 1960's has been consistently in favour has been the Foreign Office, who institutionally has seen Europe both as a means of maintaining their own world influence post Suez and increasing its own influence in Whitehall as the EU grew in power. The UK

---

[61] Lyons, Gerald, The London Mayor's economic adviser speaking at the Bruges Group/ Bloomberg conference, London 25th September 2014.

[62] European Commission, *Standard Eurobarometer 81,* Public Opinion Analysis Sector, Spring 2014

[63] Camps, Miriam, *Britain and the European Community 1955-1963*, Princeton, 1964, p. 4.

[64] Urwin, Derek, *The Community of Europe*, London, 1964, p. 46.The Prime Minister of the time, Attlee, told the Commons that "We refuse to accept the principle that the most vital economic forces of this country should be handed over to an authority that is utterly undemocratic and is responsible to nobody".

has indeed played a key role in some defining stages in the EU, notably the single market and Eastern European expansion. However, the authorities appear to have been unprepared when unintended or unexpected consequences of "good " developments, such as the SEA, also results in "bad " implications such as the growing importance of QMV and the Delors logic that a single market meant a single currency. Thus while the UK has often been very influential, as we will see it has often faced the power axis of France, Germany and a sympathetic and ambitious Commission with different ultimate goals.

The British did play a leading role in the formation of the European Free Trade Association in 1960 of 7 non EEC countries (EFTA). This was limited to free trade between members, but was not a customs union of the type the EEC was attempting to develop (common tariffs on imports from outside the block, no tariffs within), or had any objectives to form strong central institutions or any longer term objectives. The British foreign policy background to the formation of EFTA and its restriction to non EEC membership is illuminating. Negotiations began as the Treaty of Rome came into place in 1957 and was hoped to include EEC and non EEC members in a free trade group which would weaken the importance of the institutions the EEC was forming and ensure no tariff restrictions for imports to the UK from the Commonwealth. The British having held a "stand –offish attitude " to the Messina talks[65] were now attempting to share in the, now recognised, rapid economic growth of Europe and obtain some political influence, while avoiding the awkward issues of supranationalism and relationships with the Commonwealth.[66] By its failure to enlist the EEC members, it failed to be of significance as the eventual group were not important trade partners for the UK.

By the early 1960's it was evident that the countries in the EEC were the most economically successful, while the symbolic 1963 Treaty of Friendship between France and Germany showed that political relations had improved. Britain's own economic performance was now markedly weaker than the EEC countries, as it suffered from inferior trade access to the most dynamic economic bloc and had serious structural weaknesses in its balance of payments position. The EEC began to be seen as part of the modernisation strategy for British industry. It was, however, a dramatic change in policy when the Conservative Government applied to join the EEC in 1961. This about turn also reflected the humiliation of Suez and the resulting recognition that the UK needed Europe to bolster its own international position and relationship with the USA, who wanted the UK to engage more closely with Europe. However, France and Charles De Gaulle ensured that Britain's application was not accepted. In a statement on 14th January 1963 he said that Britain:

"is in effect insular, maritime, and linked through its trade, markets and food supply to very diverse and often very distant countries; she pursues essentially industrial activities and only slightly agricultural ones…..in short the nature, structure and economic context of England differs profoundly from the other states of the Continent."

It is difficult not to accept that he had a point. Despite the importance of American support for the growing prosperity of Europe, De Gaulle also stressed in later remarks his concern that Britain would act as a Trojan Horse for US influence in Europe and did not see itself as a European power. The adoption of American Polaris missiles to maintain the UK's independent deterrent was deeply unhelpful to claiming otherwise. There was indeed a dilemma for the UK that while it desired the economic stimulus that the EEC could provide, it could not easily divorce itself from its American and Commonwealth links and thus did not seek membership at any cost.

The economic challenges and declinism attitude of the 1960's and early 70's did see a consensus develop in favour of joining the Common Market, but as early as Hugh Gaitskell's speech to the Labour conference in 1962, there was a cautioning of the aspirations of the founding fathers of

---

[65] Liddle, p. 4
[66] Liddle, p. 4-5.

political union, majority voting and of a future European Parliament that appears prophetic today. The Labour party was divided on the benefits of joining with their economic focus primarily towards new mechanisms of state intervention and labour relations. On the right, Enoch Powell made the point that the unique problem of Parliament's assent to EEC membership represented a pre commitment to future laws introduced by European treaties, of which it could have no current knowledge. Again, this resonates today.

Outside the economic and constitutional debates, there is a theme in the 1960's held by Labour politicians such as Jenkins and Crosland that chimes with attitudes later in the New Labour years. It was that Europe was modern and progressive and rejected nationalism and that Britain should join to ditch its imperial illusions and commit to the European social model.

The UK Joins

It was only in 1973 with de Gaulle departed that Edward Heath was able to take the UK into the EEC alongside Ireland and Denmark. Britain was in a poor bargaining position and the terms of membership were criticised. Belief in Britain's diplomatic, economic and political decline were so firmly held that membership at almost any price was deemed necessary. Heath had explained that the EEC would entail " a sharing and an enlargement of individual national sovereignties in the general interest ", but there was " no question of any erosion of essential national sovereignty"[67]. It was reiterated in the 1975 referendum explanatory leaflet that no important EEC decisions could be made without the agreement of a British minister answerable to Parliament. The "Luxembourg Compromise", that had been endorsed at Heath's first summit, was seen to hold sway.

Powell's general hostility to Heath and the agreement he had negotiated led him to leave the Conservative's and encourage voters to vote Labour. His popularity may well have swung the balance and led to Wilson's Labour taking office in 1974.[68] Wilson, weakened by his unexpected defeat in 1970, faced a party divided on the issue of Europe and had felt he had no option when in opposition but to argue against membership on "Tory "terms. Sixty nine Labour MP's had voted in favour of membership in 1971 in defiance of a three line whip, the largest post-war rebellion until the 2003 Iraq vote. Back in power in 1974, Wilson managed the division by calling for a referendum after renegotiation and allowing his party members to follow their consciousness's. Chancellor Helmut Schmidt visited the Labour party conference to plead with Labour to stay in, although much later he came to the conclusion that De Gaulle had been correct to block UK entry.[69] It is widely acknowledged that the renegotiation was largely cosmetic and cynically executed by Wilson, but included "triumphs" such as higher quotas for cheap New Zealand lamb and butter. The Daily Mail warned that Britain's food supply would run out if we left and no national newspaper supported the exit camp. The referendum was won in 1975 on a two to one majority. As with the 2015 Scottish referendum, economic wellbeing held sway. However, it served to damage the UK relationships in Europe and continued to split the Labour party on Europe until the New Labour era. It led to Labour calling for withdrawal from Europe in its 1984 manifesto and one of the issues leading to the departure of the "Gang of Four ", including Jenkins, to form the SDP in 1981.

This initial period of membership demonstrated many of the characteristics of the UK's engagement up to today. A dominance of domestic party political implications in decision making and the ability of Europe to critically divide parties, a focus on the economic implications of Europe as a trade Zone and a general reluctance to discuss in polite society the sovereignty implications of Europe's

---

[67] Charter, David, *Europe in or Out*, London 2014, p. 109.

[68] Cash, William, Bruges Group speech, London 22 November 2014. Just before his death Powell told Sir William Cash MP that he was mistaken in leaving the Conservative Party and should have attempted to change its European policy from within.

[69] Mourlon-Druol, E, *European leaders want the UK to stay*, www.bruegel.org, sourced 21 May 2015. Interview in 2010 when realising that Thatcher and Wilson were very different from Heath.

direction of travel. The UK may have voted to join the Common Market, but as demonstrated by Gaitskell and Powell in the 1960's, the possible implications were clear at an early stage and the pro Europe case was built on concealing it. As the pro Europe Labour politician Roy Hattersley said in 2000:

"What we did throughout all those years, all the Europeans, was say, let's not risk making fundamental changes by telling the whole truth, let's do it through public relations rather than real proselytising...spin the argument rather than expose the argument....Joining the EEC did involve significant loss of sovereignty but by telling the British people that was not involved, I think the rest of the argument was prejudiced for the next 20 or 30 years."[70]

There are indeed few British politicians who have ever engaged with the vision of Europe as an idealistic project.

The 1974 renegotiation had proved a shock to the UK's partners and soon the UK acquired the reputation as an awkward partner. It did not support the development of the European Monetary system of managed currency movements, launched in 1979. It pursued from the late 1970's until settlement under Margaret Thatcher at the Treaty of Fontainebleau in 1984, a grievance over its net contribution as, at the time, the second poorest member of the EEC. The grievance arose from the importance of CAP subsidies which, with a small agricultural sector, Britain did not benefit from. The injustice was valid, but the forcefulness of Thatcher in pursuing the case was unhelpful to the UK's relationship. According to diplomat Sir Christopher Meyer, who served in Brussels in the 1980's "The UK was loathed within the Commission".[71]

The toughness of Thatcher's approach to European negotiation won her support domestically, but the middle phase of her period was dominated by the big push for the Single Market, which reflected the government's own free market thinking. It was an opportunity to play a leadership role enthusiastically supported by Business, but she as many others throughout Europe, failed to anticipate the momentum it would provide to integration with the Commission under the leadership of Jacques Delors. Thatcher set out her different version for Europe in the famous Bruges speech in September 1988. She said "We have not successfully rolled back the frontiers of the state in Britain only to see them re-imposed at a European level with a European superstate exercising a new dominance from Brussels". It had followed Delors speech to the TUC on the need for European wide social action that had recruited the UK union movement as allies. Two competing visions of Europe were now represented in UK politics, reflecting the free market and social democratic philosophy of Europe, which was to increasingly divide the Conservatives and unify Labour, who were now moving to accept the model of business friendly social democracy.

Delors also pushed the argument that the logic of the single market called for a single currency which led to internal cabinet rows over the Exchange Rate Mechanism (ERM) and the ultimate objective of a single currency. The proposed first stage of the ERM caused convulsions in British politics with Thatcher focussed on the loss of sovereignty (control over interests rates) and in conflict with her pro Europe Foreign Secretary (Howe) and Chancellor (Lawson), the latter who saw it as a useful inflation anchor. Thatcher and others of her generation who had experienced the war had also a deep concern about German dominance in Europe. One of Thatcher's favourite and likeminded ministers, Nick Ridley, was forced to resign after an interview in The Spectator commented that joint monetary policy "is all a German racket designed to take over the whole of Europe, it must be thwarted".[72] Both Howe and Lawson later resigned and she was cornered to join in 1990 by the new Chancellor John Major. Tying in Sterling at what proved to be too high an exchange rate contributed to the deep recession in the UK, public rows between Chancellor Lamont

---

[70] Charter, pp. 109-110.

[71] Meyer, Christopher, https:// twitter.com/sirsocks , sourced on 24 October 2014.

[72] Lawson, Dominic, "Speaking for England", in *The Spectator,* 14 July 1990

and the Bundesbank, and the eventual ejection of Sterling from the ERM in September 1992. To further worsen att tudes in government, in 1993 the Working Time Directive was introduced. Britain had opted out of the Maastricht Social Chapter but it was introduced in the UK under a different legal route, health and safety law, which was approved by QMV 11-1 with only the UK objecting. With the support of ECJ rulings it has had a large impact on working hour rules in the UK.

New Labour

Combined with Thatcher's forced removal and the party splits arising from the Maastricht Treaty approval by her successor John Major, the humiliation of ejection undermined the government's reputation for economic competence and meant the Conservatives became predominantly a Eurosceptic party. This was best defined in opposition from 1997 by William Hague as "In Europe, but not ruled by Europe". However, with the country's economic performance much improved and with Business pro European, the political balance moved to the pro EU social democratic agenda. The BBC, reflecting its liberal outlook, led the orientation with the narrative presented of it being favourable to be in the European "fast lane" to integration rather than "slow lane" [73]. It was consistent with the new Labour project of modernising social democratic politics and the Labour government in its first year opted in to the Social Chapter and began a process of giving up UK rebates won by Thatcher, in return for undefined CAP reform.

Tony Blair alongside Edward Heath are the two Prime Ministers who were unapologetically enthusiastic about Europe. Under his leadership the UK was a driver for the expansion to include the eastern European nations, partially to lessen Franco-German dominance, and also the deepening of the Single Market. In 1999 Blair followed Heath in winning the Charlemagne Prize for his contribution to European integration. His acceptance speech gave the opportunity to lay out his vision for Europe, of working together to meet the next global challenge of Asia, to resolve the UK's ambivalence towards Europe and that indeed it was patriotic to be pro-European. Where Blair differed from many enthusiasts is that he saw the demos in Europe as arising principally from the Council of Ministers and the democratic mandate of national leaders. The UK was a strong promoters of reforming the institutions of the EU, of streamlining the Commission and implementing subsidiarity. Through the EU Constitution and Lisbon process the UK played an important role, but ultimately with only success in the Council reforms. Blair's failure to stifle the increased power of the European Parliament has proven not to be in the UK's interests and will make the renegotiation more difficult.

For New Labour, pro Europeanism was "deep and genuine " according to Blair's Europe advisor, Roger Liddle, "but it's motivations lay in domestic politics, not in a clear vision of Britain's future in the EU….but as a brand of modernising social democratic politics ".[74] As with many other policy areas the evidence indeed is that, in Blair's first term, tactics to maintain maximum popularity were the most important factors. On Europe, keeping the Murdoch press onside and balancing the concerns and interests of Business were key objectives. Thus the Social Chapter implications were kept limited to keep Business content. Unfortunately, Business enthusiasm for the Euro and Blair's wish to support the process ran into the double obstacles of the Murdoch press and Gordon Brown. Blair was forced to retreat on his support for the Euro project when The Sun described him as "the most dangerous man in Britain". Gordon Brown ensured he had control over any decision to join by tying the matter to five economic tests that were malleable. Brown and the Treasury remained greatly influenced by "Black Wednesday", especially as Labour had supported joining the ERM. A requirement to put any recommendation on the Euro to a referendum was a concession made in the face of the opposition from the popular press and the Conservatives, proving again the priority of

---

[73] In 2005 two independent reports had found the BBC guilty of "cultural and unintentional bias"
[74] Liddle, p. xxiii

domestic considerations. Whatever the reason, from the moment the UK opted out of the Euro in 1991, keeping out of the euro has been probably the best strategic judgment the UK has made since 1945. As Blair became overwhelmed by the fall out from Iraq, which also worsened relations with France, Europe moved down the agenda. Also of significance is evidence that the Blair/Brown divisions reduced the UK's effectiveness in EU negotiations as it severely hindered a coordinated UK position.[75] The Conservative Party also upset the major European centre right parties and reportedly reduced its influence by leaving the EPP Parliamentary Group to form a new grouping, the ECR.

By the time the Lisbon Treaty was signed, Blair had been replaced by Brown, who missed the formal signing ceremony and signed the Treaty alone from the other leaders in an unsuccessful attempt to lower its profile. This reflected the attempts to downplay its significance in the face of a Eurosceptic outcry and a Conservative commitment for a referendum on its terms, which it later had to drop once it passed into UK law. The more significant Maastricht Treaty had, of course, been passed by a Conservative government without a referendum.

One enduring British problem where the EU's development has been of assistance has been Northern Ireland, where in 2007 power sharing was eventually implemented. The EU provided Eire with a new status out of the shadows of the UK and contributed greatly to its economic and social development, including the provision of special assistance.

2010 onwards

By waiving the seven year transition rules for the movement of Labour, Blair, in his enthusiasm for Eastern European expansion, invigorated Euroscepticism in a completely unanticipated way. Hundreds of thousands of east Europeans unexpectedly took advantage of their right to live and work in Britain with very significant economic, social and political consequences. When the coalition government was formed in 2010, it appeared that a low profile, non assertive pro European consensus had been formed. The "middle ground "of politics was to grumble about the EU but to accept it was generally in the UK's interests. The Lisbon treaty had been passed as a hoped for final stage in the EU's powers and institutions and David Cameron had famously been reported to say that the Conservatives should stop "banging on about Europe", which was seen as of great concern to a small minority in his party and country. The game changers have, of course, been the Euro crisis, the impact of immigration in a recession, a realisation by many ministers once in government as to how restrictive European regulations were on their freedom of action and, most recently, the growing importance of UKIP. In 2011 the EU Act was passed to provide for a referendum in the event of substantial additional powers being passed to Brussels and can be viewed as a mechanism by the Conservative leadership to close the issue down. This produced a revolt of 81 Conservative MP's calling for an immediate in-out referendum, the largest post war revolt and much larger than occurred over Maastricht. Since then the rise of UKIP has led to further concessions, notably Conservative policy for a renegotiation in areas outlined in Cameron's January 2013 Bloomberg speech and a resulting 2017 in -out referendum on membership.

Earlier, in July 2011 the Chancellor, George Osborne, commented on the" remorseless logic" of the Euro area nations undertaking greater fiscal integration and that the UK would not stand in the way of what the inner core had to do to save the Euro.[76] It was not commented on at the time, but this statement can be viewed as a reversal of British foreign policy for at least the past 50 years. Britain was now prepared to support a more politically integrated Continent which she would not be part

[75] David Frost , former senior civil servant, speaking at Open Europe conference on 16 February 2015.
[76] Giles, Chris & Parker, "George, Osborne urges Eurozone to get a grip", in the *Financial Times,* 20 July 2011

of. It is also perhaps symbolic of the reluctant necessity to finally confront the political issues that, only from 2013 and Cameron's Bloomberg Speech, has any mainstream party sought to remove the totemic phrase "ever closer union. "

At an April 2015 Chatham House debate, the consensus of the distinguished panel was that the UK's influence in Europe had never been weaker and it was unclear what reforms were being sought. It was remarked that Cameron was referred to by German speakers in Council meetings by a term translated into English as "the alien body".[77] Certainly Cameron has approached the EU on a transactional basis and has changed his position on the basis of UKIP and Eurosceptic pressure. Those who criticise Cameron conveniently excuse the motivations of others able to hide behind their enthusiasm for the EU. Chancellor Merkel had been initially been against Juncker's appointment, but his own lobbying for support had attracted the support of powerful German media interests (due to his willingness to investigate Google), resulting in Merkel's U turn and the humiliation of Cameron. The unexpected decisiveness of the general election result appears, however, to have markedly increased Cameron's authority with warm noises of co-operation emerging from many European and EU leaders.

Implications of the UK's attitude to the EU

According to Liddle one of the weaknesses of the British political system is that it is "not easy to persuade British politicians to network across Europe". Many EU matters are long term consensus projects not attractive to ministers thinking of the next job and hoping to avoid a toxic headline over Europe.[78] European style political consensus building is also not as familiar in a UK political system where coalition politics has not been the norm. Moreover, politics remains Westminster centric with a low profile for most MEP's. This perhaps means that loss of authority to Brussels has been under the noses of successive governments. In October 2014 a coalition government paper sponsored by the Liberal Democrats called for "a step change in how as a country we engage at EU level " with" systematic long term alliance building by government".[79] This is a familiar refrain illustrating the UK's weaknesses in its dealings with the EU. Another drawback is the reduced Foreign Office resources in individual EU nations which hinders efforts to promote the UK's position and build alliances, which could have implications for the renegotiation.

This traditional lack of engagement is reflected by the proportionately small number of UK officials working in the EU institutions. While Britain has 12.7 % of the EU population, the proportion of officials working in the Commission in 2013 was 4.3%, compared with 8.4% from Germany and 9.6% from France.[80] This is perhaps one factor in what retired diplomat Sir Christopher Meyer describes as the "longstanding and exquisite sensitivity of the EU Commission to French concerns"[81]. Moreover, upcoming retirements will shortly reduce Britain's senior representation in Brussels further. The Europe Minister, David Lidington has stated that the UK lacks a strategic approach to

---

[77] Professor Timothy Garton Ash of Oxford University speaking at "Challenges and Choices for the UK" at Chatham House on 16 March 2015. The general tone of the speakers was so pro Europe that it was hardly a balanced debate however. Issues such as the impact of the eurocrisis on unemployment do not seem to have troubled the groupthink.
[78] Liddle, p. 95
[79] Moore, Michael, *Doing Business Across Europe: A new engagement,* Deputy Prime Minister's Office, HMG, 2014
[80] Pancevski, Bojan, "German Invasion cuts Britons out of top jobs in *The Sunday Times",* 24 November 2014
[81] Meyer, https:// twitter.com/sirsocks, sourced on 25 October 2014.

the use of secondments to EU institutions, which is an important networking strength for pursuing national interests the UK is lacking.[82] It is thus a legitimate concern that UK politicians and officials will be particularly challenged in the renegotiation process.

As indicated above by reported attitudes to Cameron, the UK's strong Euroscepticism is also widely viewed as causing difficulties in alliance building with other nations and relations with the EU institutions, even when the UK's viewpoint has support. It is well established that other nations are comfortable in hiding behind the UK in opposition to particular EU initiatives. Germany has had no such difficulty when she pursues her own interests. This guides the UK's renegotiation efforts towards initiatives that can have broad based appeal.

A summary of the range of UK attitudes to the UK today

In 2013, Cameron's Bloomberg speech summed up many of the issues facing the EU from a Eurosceptic. Its lack of competitiveness and declining economic power, its democratic deficit and bloated institutions that ignored the principle of subsidiarity, the doubtful relevance of a one dimensional bloc and thus the inapplicability of "ever closer union" and lastly the lack of a single European demos. "It is national parliaments which are, and will remain, the true source of democratic legitimacy and accountability in the EU". The EU needed reform.[83] It is ironic that the Conservative Party, which initially proposed joining the Common Market, took the UK into membership and approved the defining Single European Act and Maastricht treaty (without a referendum), is now primarily Eurosceptic. Certainly the EU institutions are predominately Social Democratic in their culture.

We can identify the following alternative strands of opinion in the UK which will be opinion formers in renegotiation or exit decisions. The pro and anti-camps are, of course, confused by the conflicting social democratic and free market impulses of the EU.

The "Left", the BBC and the Unions

The strong emphasis on workers' rights in Europe has meant that the left wing and the Labour Party remain strong EU supporters. The TUC in particular opposes the repatriation of powers as a danger to the social dimension of the single market. The Left is philosophically attracted to the "Great State" concept of Europe and its distrust of Anglo Saxon capitalism. NGO's such as Friends of the Earth have proved to be very effective lobbyists in Brussels in influencing policy and the legal status given to the Charter of Fundamental Rights has encouraged new rulings to develop human rights.

In some respects, however, the Left is contradictory and confused. Strangely absent from mainstream Left opinion at present is any concern that the EU can be seen as supportive of powerful big business and their lobbyists. This critique is provided by the free market opponents of the EU. Also, the UK Left is largely mute in highlighting the impact of the Euro crisis on living conditions and unemployment in countries such as Greece and Spain which is providing a narrative for both anti austerity protests and the requirement for EU reform. For domestic public sector concerns, the unions are opposed to aspects of TTIP, which aligns them with the protectionist sympathies of many southern European socialists. The future may well see a growing split on the Left of their views on

---

[82] Clifford Chance,TheCityUK, *A legal assessment of the UK's relationship with the EU- A Financial Services Perspective*, London, 2014, p. 13

[83] Cameron, *David, Bloomberg speech*, 23 January 2013, www.gov.uk/government/s[eeches/eu-speech-at-bloomberg, sourced 13 August 2015

the EU, but for the 2015 election the Labour party refused to countenance a referendum or the possibility of a new terms of membership specifically for the UK, but has joined the consensus for the need for reform and the promotion of growth initiatives, which reflect much of the Brussels consensus.[84] The 2015 Labour manifesto calls for a "red card " procedure for national Parliaments to be introduced and reforms in the UK's interests, without mention of the EU's interests. In a recent poll 58% of Labour voters wished to stay in the EU compared with 39% of Conservative voters[85].

Big Business and the City.

Multinational companies and the major City institutions have been major beneficiaries from the Single Market and are alarmed by the uncertainty of any renegotiation. They also focus on the benefit of bloc negotiation of Free Trade Agreements. In a 2013 CBI report the current status quo (or indeed further integration) was presented as much more preferable to leaving the EU.[86] It is noticeable that business attitudes tend to ignore the political aspects of the EU and the likelihood that "anti-business" views of some EU politicians will set aspects of the European policy agenda. The "City" viewpoint, of course, reflects many non UK institutions who are members of the CBI and CityUK. Smaller UK institutions, particularly in the fund management industry and "hedge funds" which draw much of their assets from outside Europe, are much less enthusiastic, reflecting the onerous AIFMD regulations. These are widely recognised as very severe, given the industry was not a cause of the financial crisis and reflected the post crisis punishment culture in the Commission and European Parliament.

Other Business Interests.

Without the resources of large companies, smaller companies are also much less enthusiastic. Lobby Groups such as Business for Britain focus on the cost of regulation and its impact in restricting competition. The failure to implement service sector Single Market access is also emphasised. The British Chamber of Commerce tracks attitudes among UK businesses to the EU. Its Q3 2014 Euro Business Barometer of 3500 businesses indicated that a majority wanted to stay in the EU but with a substantial return of powers. 59% viewed withdrawal as negative. At its 2015 conference it supported a reformed Europe and warned against a euro dominated EU.

The Judiciary

With the expansion of the remit of the ECJ into the field of human rights, members of the Supreme Court are concerned that the lack of a written constitution in the UK and the supremacy of the 1972 European Communities Act provides few limits to the dominance of EU law and the ECJ.

Parliament

Is concerned by the diminished ability to influence and scrutinise legislation due to QMV in the Council and the "trilogue" process of negotiation between the Council, Commission and European Parliament.

The "Right", most of the press and anti Europeans.

---

[84] Shadow Foreign Secretary's speech at Chatham House on 17 January 2014 confirmed Labour's position
[85]see Pickard, 2015
[86] see CBI, *Our Global Future*, London, 2013.

Share all the EU concerns above, together with the issue of immigration and the poor economic performance of Europe. They would prefer to form new trade alliances with the Commonwealth and NAFTA. Withdrawal from the EU would be preferable to remaining in an unreformed EU. Free marketers also bring attention to the regulatory nature of the EU which by definition protects incumbents and hinders disruptive entrants. A recent examples is an EU attempt to control electronic cigarettes.

While Eurosceptic UK opinion is largely pro free market this contrasts with the powerful anti EU forces in France and southern Europe which are largely protectionist and against market reform. This clearly confuses the EU "reform" agenda.

Would there be a consensus view of what direction the UK would follow outside the EU?

In our examination of UK attitudes to the EU we have identified a multitude of opinions. While it may well be possible to develop a fairly broad consensus as the attractiveness of increasing national control over policy making and thus greater democratic accountability, there is much less likelihood of an ideological consensus of how the UK would prosper after Brexit. From a free market viewpoint, low levels of regulation, freer trade (meaning greater competition from Asia) and continued inward migration would be economically desirable, but would not be acceptable to many. A question far from being settled is thus what would the UK actually want for its future after withdrawal, a free market or protectionism?

THE ECONOMIC COST-BENEFIT ANALYSIS

We have established the substantial loss of sovereignty (notional and real), to a new form of shared sovereignty with weak democratic controls. It is not possible to put an economic number on the value of national level policy making and democratic accountability, but we will now contrast the democratic deficit with the economic case. A populist approach would bring attention to the EU "gravy train" and the £10-15bn cost of membership (see "The Consequences of the Brussels decision making process " above). However the actual sums are modest in relation to the size of the UK economy, and so below we will concentrate on the bigger picture.

Trade and the Single Market

The Facts: The EU is a Customs Union which aims to eliminate all barriers to internal trade while negotiating its trading relationships with external nations as a uniform bloc, preventing the UK from entering bilateral Free Trade Agreements (FTA's). UK exports of goods and services to the EU accounted for 42% of total exports in 2012, a decline from 48% in 2000. If the "Rotterdam-Antwerp " conduit effect of re-export outside the EU is ignored the total rises to approximately 50%, which is the "headline" figure often quoted. UK exports to the rest of the world are growing more rapidly and in 2012 overtook EU trade. The UK is less dependent on EU trade than most other EU states and after the EU the UK's largest trading partner is the US with total trade levels at 43% of the EU total. However the UK's trade is not well represented in the world's regions with the most economic growth potential in Asia and South America.

While the EU is by far the biggest destination of UK trade in goods, the volume of export of services is much lower. Services account for 71% of EU GDP, but only about 23% and 22% of the EU's internal exports and imports respectively.

For all EU trade, Germany is the UK's main trading partner followed by the Netherlands and France. The UK runs a large deficit in manufactured goods trade and relies heavily on the export of services. 39% of all UK- EU trade is in sectors such as chemicals, food and beverages and cars where the EU is protected from imports from outside the EU by relatively high EU tariffs. Food and beverages have the highest average tariff of over 20% and ranging up to 57% for dairy products. In the car industry (8% of total trade), there is an average EU tariff of 10% as well as significant non-tariff barriers.

Successive World Trade Organisation rounds have significantly reduced tariffs to the extent that about 50% of world merchandise trade is already subject to Zero tariff rates. In 1973 the average industrial tariff was over 10% but is now less than 3%. Non-tariff barriers can continue to block or impede trade however.[87]

The European Economic Area (EEA) is comprised of Norway, Iceland and Liechtenstein and the members of the EU and allows the non EU members to participate in the internal market by accepting almost all EU laws on the internal market except those relating to agriculture and fisheries. Norway, Iceland and Liechtenstein along with Switzerland constitute EFTA (European Free Trade Association) and was formed by those countries not willing to join the EEC. The UK and other countries were members until they joined the EEC. EFTA have arranged as a bloc free trade agreements with other nations outside the EU. Switzerland is not a member of the EEA but participates in the Single Market via bilateral agreements with the EU.

---

[87] Charter, p. 122 and Stewart-Brown, Ronald, *Discussion Paper- UK Trade Statistics,* October 2013, www.tprc.org.uk , sourced 15 December 2014.

The Single Market has been at the core of the EU's development and its presentation as a major contributor to the UK's economic prosperity has been the key rationale for the UK's membership. The expansionary interpretation of the Four Freedoms and the removal of barriers to the Freedoms has, for example in the area of a EU citizens right of residence anywhere in the EU, extended the boundaries of EU powers. In this section we will, however, concentrate on the narrower economic implications of trade patterns and the Single Market. It is often noted that the UK has brought a liberalising impact to the EU through its sponsorship of free trade, the Single Market and the privatisation agenda, the latter of which the Commissioners forced other member states to follow in the late 1990's. The UK has thus helped balance the more protectionist attitude of some EU members, notably in Southern Europe.

In the twenty years before the UK joined the EEC, the proportion of UK trade with the original 6 member nations rose from 13% to just 21%. In the 20 years following joining, UK trade with the same group more than doubled to 44%.[88] This reflected the common standards and rules introduced to smooth trade and, as a customs union, the common external tariffs which deterred imports from outside the EU.

Outside this proportionate increase in trade with the EU there has also been a general increase in world trade due to globalisation and the general lowering of trade barriers through the World Trade Organisation (WTO) rounds. World trade has grown faster than global output and between 1960-2007 world trade tripled, while world economic output only doubled.[89] Thus we have seen a regional economic integration within the EU at the same time as growing trade between advanced and emerging economies. The Single Market has encouraged what the CBI describe as a new model of globalisation, with cross border intra industry regional supply chains creating complex interdependence and integration. Around half of the UK's imports from the EU consists of intermediates that are imbedded in UK products for sale at home or re-exported.[90]

In recent years the proportion of UK trade with the EU has begun to decline reflecting globalisation and the stronger economic growth of other regions. On current trends by 2017 and allowing 10% for the "Rotterdam Effect", goods and services exports to the EU are expected to be just 37.5%. The economic case for the Customs Union and the Single Market can no longer be taken for granted.

To determine the Single Market benefits of the EU to the UK we have to consider the following

- The impact of the EU on our trade relationships with the rest of the world.

- The benefits and costs of being a member of the EU Single Market.

EU-Global Trade relationships

The Geopolitical Aspect

Before the UK joined the EU, trade policy was a key aspect of foreign policy, which has passed to the EU. This has a classic shared sovereignty trade off in that, to the extent the EU's 28 members can agree, trade agreements and sanctions are more powerful. Because trade agreements have moved beyond tariff reductions to how business operates, it is even more a key foreign policy tool and the

[88] Charter, p. 124
[89] Centre for European Reform, *The Economic Consequences of leaving the EU*, London, 2014, p. 10
[90] CBI, p. 38

economic battleground for the "West " versus its rivals, whoever makes the rules in economic relationships has a distinct advantage.

In another example of foreign policy impact, EU trade sanctions on Iran and most recently Russia have demonstrated efficacy and, in the case of Russia, probably ensured that nations such as Hungary participated at all. In current negotiations with the US, measures to improve EU energy security via access to US shale gas is part of the EU objectives. Finally, EU trade representation avoids the UK being subject to individually discriminatory trade sanctions, for example by Argentina, as such measures would be considered an attack on all EU states. From a foreign policy viewpoint, therefore, the EU's role in trade policy can be more potent in advancing the UK's national interests. This is developed further in "The EU relationship and UK foreign policy" below.

Negotiating Trade Deals

The huge increase in world trade has been assisted by the successive rounds of WTO liberalisation, but in recent years this has ground to a halt with the very slow progress of the Doha round of talks which began in 2001. The EU has indeed been criticised for focusing on the multilateral process while other key nations such as the US pushed on to negotiate direct free trade agreements (FTA). The growing importance of supply-chain trade has meant that the tariff and quota focus of the WTO is much less effective and requires a negotiation process more suited to bilateral negotiations between countries or regional blocs. Thus regional trade deals including matters such as regulatory harmonisation, intellectual property right protection and customs procedures (eg avoidance of double product testing), are now seen as necessary and effective. It is through membership of the EU that the UK has participated in globally recognised standards and participate in over 30 FTA's including with Canada, Singapore and South Korea. Even though the UK's priorities are not always met the CBI concludes that it "would be difficult to envisage how the UK could succeed in breaking down regulatory barriers to trade with a major country to the same extent in unilateral negotiations".[91]

Thus although it could be argued that the UK has conceded regulatory sovereignty in having to meet EU standards, this would seem to be largely illusionary, given that the EU has an important role in determining global product standards, which the UK would likely to have to conform with in export markets and is able to influence through EU membership. It is worth recalling that the UK although the sixth largest economy accounts for only 1% of the world's population and about 3% of GDP. The power of the EU bloc is such that in the case of the EEA members, to obtain access to the EU markets, the non EU members such as Norway are required to implement EU regulations without a strong voice to influence them. In the case of Switzerland with approximately 120 bilateral sectorial agreements with the EU, regulations must also comply (a considerable proportion of EU trade law is written into Swiss law). Thus the danger is that the UK could suffer from "regulation without representation "outside the EU. On the other hand Switzerland avoids the EU social and employment legislation of the Single Market, but does have to follow rules of origin or resultant tariffs for its imports from outside the EU, accepts open border immigration from the EU and pays a contribution to the EU of about 60% of the UK's.[92]

The fact remains that because of the divergent national interests the EU has been slow in negotiating FTA's. Thus while Switzerland and New Zealand have secured FTA's with China, this is not on the horizon for the EU and means the UK will continue to face trade barriers with this crucial market for future growth. It is also noteworthy that 5 million population Norway has a significant independent voice in world trade standard negotiations where it has significant interests, such as

---

[91] CBI, p. 12

[92] Lyons, Gerard, *The Europe Report: A Win-Win situation*, Mayor of London, August 2014, Appendix

food, while the UK must largely work through the EU with its multitude of national interests.[93] However the Norwegian political establishment has no love for the current arrangements with the EU as it has to accept the most costly EU regulations without representation. The choice for the UK would seem to be, get better deals via EU trade deals or by leaving the EU work independently and have a weaker bargaining position, but have the flexibility to arrange deals much quicker or in circumstances where the EU cannot reach agreement. However in this scenario the UK would still have to meet EU rules to export to the EU, its largest trading partner.

The potential deal with the US (TTIP- Transatlantic Trade and Investment Partnership), is viewed as a crucial indicator of the EU's ability to represent the UK's interests, compared for example with Switzerland's ability to agree its own bilateral trade arrangements. The US is the UK's second largest trading partner. The negotiations reflect the complexity of modern trade negotiations. Because conventional tariffs are now so low, the key barriers to trade are cross border/ transportation red tape and meeting EU regulatory standards based on the precautionary principle and including matters such as health and safety and environmental impact.[94] The protectionist interests of some groups, such as French farming, has been historically a restriction on reducing barriers on trade outside the EU and the European Parliament has also slowed negotiations by the requirement to obtain its approval to new FTA's and is attempts to add non trade conditions to FTA's. With adaption to globalisation being a key factor in the UK's future success, the danger of a "Fortress Europe" approach is a key concern. In matters such as food, different cultural and value viewpoints can also act as a barrier. For example, in Germany there is much public concern about GM modified US food being imported, a matter where the UK is moving to a more accommodative position and where decisions have been delegated to nation states. TTIP is the model for the scope of most trade agreements for the future in largely focusing on regulatory convergence, but if the UK's cultural and value norms differ materially from continental partners and prevent TTIP being approved, then this would be an important indicator that the EU is not the best future negotiator of the UK's interests.

The trend to global integration and regulation

A feature of globalisation is the trend to global standard setting and the danger of the reducing power of the EU as its own relative economic size declines. For example, many of the Single Market food standards result from a global body Codex Alimentarius. In the car industry regulatory standards start at the World Forum for the Harmonisation of Vehicle regulations.[95] In both cases their standards are integrated into the Single Market. So again this trend raises the question, as the sixth largest economy in the world could the UK generally promote its own interests better directly as New Zealand does, rather than having one vote in a a 28 member bloc, by forming alliances as her needs demanded ? In banking regulation, for example, the G20 already manages many issues where the UK is represented by the Bank of England. On the other hand, the EU Trade Commissioner, Cecilia Malmstrom, has defended the possible US trade deal as a means for the EU and US to work together to influence global regulatory standards after reaching agreement between themselves[96],to counter the power of the East. If the EU believes it needs to align with the US to

---

[93] Lindsell, Jonathan, *The Norwegian Way. A case study for Britain's future relationship with the EU*, Civitas, London, 2015, p. 37
[94] Pascal Lamy, former head of the WTO organisation, speaking at Chatham House on 2 June 2015 estimated that of costs of export to EU , 5% would be tariffs,10% border/container red tape and 20% meeting EU standards based on the precautionary principle.
[95] Patterson, Owen, *"An optimistic vision of the post-EU UK "*., http://www.uk2020.org.uk/wp-content/uploads/2014/10/Owen-Paterson-Europe-Speech-24-November-2014-Online.pdf ,speech given on 24 November 2014.
[96] Speech to Open Europe Conference on TTIP in Brussels 11 December 2014

have power, it somewhat puts into context the limited impact that the UK alone could have in fields such as pharmaceuticals, machinery or food.

An alternative model which may have produced a similar trade impact to the EU is the North American Free Trade Association, formed in 1994 by the US, Canada and Mexico. In fact some Republican politicians suggested that the UK would benefit from joining. The Economist magazine noted that NAFTA was the sort of arrangement the UK always wanted the EU to be, "a giant free-trade area linking sovereign countries without any common body of law, or any notion of developing a common foreign policy"[97]. Trade in NAFTA increased from $290bn at its foundation in 1993 to $1.1trillion in 2012.[38] Thus with hindsight would the UK have been better served to arrange a free trade agreement with the EU or remain in EFTA, with the liberty to make its own trading arrangements with other parties outside the association? To consider that question we must examine the customs union implications of being part of the most developed model of regional integration.

---

[97] Charter, p.129
[98] Sergie, Mohammed, *NAFTA's economic impact* ,CFR Backgrounders, www.cfr.org, sourced 3 December 2014

The Single Market

The EU's Single market development has involved the removal of tariff barriers and major efforts to remove non-tariff barriers by enforcing EU wide competition law, for example by preventing state subsidies and coordinating product regulation so exporters do not have to comply with 28 differing national rules. Budget airlines, for example, resulted from transport regulations breaking national flag carrier cartels. The EU has also been very active in investigating and sanctioning uncompetitive collusion arrangements in areas as diverse as bathroom ceramics and automotive parts. Microsoft and Intel have also faced severe sanctions for uncompetitive practices and Google and Gazprom have recently been charged. It is generally viewed as one of the EU's most successful interventions, attacking uncompetitive markets and changing the practices of both EU companies and global multinationals. One justifiable criticism is, however, that some interventions against non EU multinationals could have their motivations in a wish to protect EU companies. The recently launched investigations into Google and other internet platforms is for some driven by a wish to assist the development of EU based alternatives or protect domestic media from the disruptive impact of the internet.

The EU's measures to promote capital and labour mobility via the Single Market has also ensured cross border flows. For example 14% of workers in the UK in 2012 were born outside the UK with the proportion growing.[99] In purely economic terms these are all positive factors.

The UK has been the largest beneficiary of foreign direct Investment (FDI) into the Single Market and thus the third largest recipient after the US and China.[100] Of course many factors can account for the attractiveness of the UK as an inward investment destination including language, the open economy and the ease of starting businesses. The UK is also indeed one of the largest global exporters of capital reflecting its global perspective. However, the impact of the Single Market can be demonstrated by the fact that 60% of FDI is in services and nearly 50% in banking, the most integrated service sector. It is another measure of the impact of integration that EU direct investment in the UK has risen faster than from elsewhere, so that while in 1997 EU countries accounted for 30% of the accumulated total of investment in the UK, by 2012 it had risen to 50%.[101]

The Limitations of the Single Market

The Single Market claims to give UK business access to a market of 500 million people. However, while in physical goods trade Single Market integration driven by the ECJ has been highly successful, in the network industries and in the service economy the record is much less favourable. This is because national regulations and characteristics remain dominant. In telecoms, energy and transport, competition policy is largely operated on a national basis. Enabling network industries to operate as single integrated EU market with economies of scale could be very advantageous, but these benefits are currently largely untapped. For example, increasing electricity grid connectivity could allow the renewable energy surpluses from Spain to be exported to France and ultimately could be a way for the EU to improve its energy security. Grid integration, however, requires huge capital expenditure and has created national disputes already. This failure therefore reflects the difficulty the EU is having in furthering economically beneficial integration. More fruitful is likely to be changes to competition standards in mobile telephony which requires four providers in each individual national market, compared with China or the US which have three major national providers in much larger markets. The EU has enabled a fragmented telecoms market lacking economies of scale and reduced profitability and has failed to take into account the growing

---

[99]CBI, p. 23, quoting OECD statistics
[100]CBI, p. 24, quoting OECD statistics.
[101] Centre for European Reform, *The Economic consequences of leaving the EU*, 2014.

importance of 4G and broadband. The indications are that under pressure from Chancellor Merkel industry consolidation throughout Europe will be encouraged, but it is an example of how the EU's institutions are failing to respond effectively to innovation.

In the service economy the Single Market has also been much less successful with particular implications for the service sector dominated UK economy. While the service sector accounts for over 70% of EU GDP it only accounts for 22% of EU trade and it is accepted that "there is no truly integrated single market in services".[102] One reason for this lesser integration is that the 2006 Services Directive has not been implemented fully and in negotiation was watered down and restricted in the sectors encompassed, due to their wide diversity. Protectionism has been evident with some nations imposing economic needs tests that require businesses to prove there is demand for their services, despite this being prohibited. E commerce is also restricted, for example, by national laws on when sale discounts can be offered which causes uncertainty. Most importantly the country of origin principle, which means that service providers only need to comply with the regulations of their home states in order to provide services in others, was removed in the negotiation. According to a parliamentary committee, of the 45% of service industries covered by the directive, (which includes retail, wholesale trades and professional services), greater liberalisation could boost EU GDP by 1.8-2.3%.[103] As noted above one exception in the service sector is, however, wholesale banking which is highly integrated due to the application of the country of origin principle via the passport system bringing major benefits to the City of London.

A further significant integration weakness is the retention of Corporation Tax policy by nations. Tax rates vary markedly and a low regime has been an important factor, for example, in Eire's ability to attract US multinationals. It is perhaps the failure to create a single market in the service economy combined with remaining "border effects" (remaining non-tariff barriers, tax, energy prices, language and cultural differences) that means that trade between the states of the US is around 70% higher than between members of the EU15.[104] This puts the claims for the success and impact of the Single Market in some context, particularly for a large non continental economy such as the UK. The Single Market is far from complete.

The economic costs and benefits of the Single Market-how big is its impact?

Even though we have established that the Single Market is actually restricted in scope, UK politicians like to claim that it has been crucial to the UK economic performance. Does this stand up to analysis? The UK governments 2013 review of the Single Market analysed the economic studies of the single market and concluded that "most but not all of the studies suggest that the GDP of the EU and the UK is appreciably greater than it otherwise would be thanks to….the single market"[105] and that future gains were possible. The economic case for the benefits of economic integration arises through increased trade (and thus the benefits of specialisation and comparative advantage reducing prices, and the resultant increased innovation and productivity). However, given the Single Market restrictions, the total gains are not as dramatic as some would expect and the most extensive studies estimate EU GDP gains over the decades up to 2007 in the single digits. The most recent and wide ranging study suggested that EU GDP could be around 5% higher in 2008 than it

---

[102] Fresh Start Project, *The Single Market in Services*, www.eufreshstart.org, 2013, sourced 12 March 2015.
[103] All Party Parliamentary Group for European Reform, *Inquiry into the EU single market in services,* London, 2013.

[104] Department for Business Innovation and Skills, *The economic consequences for the UK and the EU of completing the single market,* BIS Economic Paper No. 11, February 2011.
[105] HM Government, *Review of the Balance of Competencies: The Single Market, July 2013,* Department for Business Innovation and Skills and the Foreign and Commonwealth Office, London, July 2013

otherwise would be.[106] These studies do not consider the specific benefits to the UK or the later impact of the Euro crisis or if a European free trade area of the NAFTA style could have produced similar benefits. After all, intra-regional trade flows in Asia have also dramatically increased and boosted economic growth without a "Single Market."

Perhaps economic growth statistics will support the importance of the Single Market for the UK? If we examine the economic growth statistics, in the period 1957-1973 the six original EEC members GDP grew at an average rate of 4.9% with all of them growing quickly (France 5%, Italy 5.3%, Germany 4.7%), compared with 2.8% for the UK. With the US growing at 3.8% and many other nations in the world demonstrating growth of 3.5%- 4.8%, it illustrates that it was the UK that was exceptional in its relatively poor performance due to its particular problems such as labour relations. If we then compare the period from 1980-2007 when the Single Market grew in significance, then the UK's relative performance, helped by economic reform, improved to 2.4% p.a. growth compared with 2.9 % for the USA and exceeded the 2.1% for France, 1.6% for Germany and 1.8% for Italy and matched the 2.4% for the Netherlands.[107] Other factors were clearly more important than the EU in the UK's economic performance, especially as the Continental economies are more integrated than the UK and should have seen relatively larger Single Market benefits and thus higher growth. Moreover, the better relative performance of the EEC in the period up to the early 1970's can also be partially explained by the structural changes in the main economies as their large agricultural sector modernised and labour was redeployed to more productive industrial sectors, a trend not applicable to the UK.

For the UK, studies by Eurosceptic economists have looked at the costs of integration from a UK perspective taking into account regulation, the fact that UK trade is more global[108], the cost of CAP and the benefit of alternative free trade arrangements. The 2005 report by Minford argued that the UK was 2-3% worse off while Congdon in 2012 estimated that the UK was 10% worse off because of EU membership. At the other extreme the CBI in 2014 in an empirical study of only physical trade flows with the EU concluded that trade had been boosted by 55% by membership.[109] This illustrates that the two sides approach the issue of costs and benefits from different angles.

Assessing economic developments against a non-existing counterfactual is clearly difficult, but intuitively when only approximately 14% of UK GDP is accounted for by exports to the EU then large areas of the domestic economy are bearing the costs of integration which they may not benefit from. For example, the NHS has borne significant costs due to the imposition of the European Working Time Directive. Moreover, the employee heavy service sector generally, which would be the most clearly impacted by employment legislation, is not well integrated into the Single Market. The CBI, normally a cheer leader for the EU identified a "strong business preoccupation with the extent and nature of the regulatory burden" and together with the HMG 2013 Competency review noted the following single market issues of concern to its members:[110]

- Poor implementation of EU rules in the UK, partially because our legal system requires a greater level of detail, but also reflecting "gold plating". A 2010 report found that public

[106] Boltho & Eichengreen, *The Economic Impact of European Integration,* Centre for Economic Policy Research, London, 2008

[107] see Bootle, 2014

[108] HM Treasury, *The Economic Effects of EU membership for the UK (2005)*, estimated that UK trade with EU members increased by only 7%, with 4% diverted from non EU trade, reflecting the relative openness of the UK economy and much lower than the EU averages.

[109] HM Government, *Review of the Balance of Competencies. The Single Market, July 2013,* section 3.10 and appendix.

[110] CBI, November 2013, chapter 3.An IPSOS Mori Poll quoted in the Daily Telegraph polled Directors at the UK's 500 largest companies in February 2013 with 79% of 109 responses saying the level of regulation was harming the UK economy.

procurement under the EU directive took 50% longer and was 50% more expensive than the EU average.[111] There is considerable anecdotal evidence from various industry groups to support this conclusion.

- One size fits all labour and industrial relationship systems. In particular the Temporary Agency Directive imposed "unreasonable restrictions and costs".
- Consistent Brussels challenges to the opting out provisions of the WTD and ECJ interpretations of its scope was causing "disruptive uncertainty". This was recently evidenced by a 2014 ECJ ruling on holiday pay, which could potentially increase employment costs materially in some segments where commission based pay is prevalent.
- A problem with enforcement of Single Market rules with standards applied differently with national regulators, other than in northern Europe and the Netherlands, using flexibility in EU measures to delay introduction. This included the services, e commerce and data protection directives and generally placed UK firms at a competitive disadvantage, especially as legal enforcement processes are not acting as a deterrent due to the slow ECJ process.

Of course, as the CBI argue, the extent of the additional EU burden depends on the likely degree of standalone UK regulation and a recent review by the Mayor of London[112] has confirmed the prevailing view that the savings by a distinct UK regulatory environment are unlikely to be large, especially if the UK must adopt EU or global standards to trade abroad. More regulation is a fact of life in all modern developed economies and Westminster politicians and civil servants are just as capable as the European Parliament of introducing red tape. We cannot blame the EU for much of our planning system, for example. Even with EU regulation a study finds the UK the tenth most competitive economy in the world,[113] while the OECD labour market protection index shows that the UK economy's labour flexibility is broadly equivalent to Canada and the USA and much greater than continental Europe despite the efforts of Brussels. This flexibility in the UK labour market helps explain why the UK's job creation record since the Great Recession is much stronger than other member economies and contrasts with the 35 hour working week restrictions in France.

Irrespective of the impact of the Single Market the open UK economy has also been a beneficiary of the trends of globalisation and economic liberalisation which occurred from the 1980's. This again casts doubts on the value of a highly integrated Single Market as the old presumption that the EU was founded on, that larger countries are more economically efficient, is greatly challenged by how the world has changed to allow small countries to compete. Most poor nations that have experienced rapid economic growth in the era since the EU was formed have been extensively involved in international trade, including the UK's former key trading partners in the Commonwealth.[114] In other words, the advantages and economies of scale of a big state creating its own free trade area are lost by the generally much increased global integration/lowering of barriers. As discussed above, in important network industries where economies of scale through EU could have greatly benefited all member nations, notably energy, progress has been very slow. None of the above is suggesting that the benefits of the Single Market are appreciably better than other free trade arrangements which would likely involve lower costs for non-exporting sectors and less loss of sovereignty.

Our overall conclusion from the economic statistics is that the economic case for the UK's membership of the EU is not proven, but only one of a variety of influences effecting individual nations including international competitiveness and the major economic gains from globalisation

---

[111] PwC, *Public Procurement in Europe, a study for the European Union*, 2011
[112] Lyons, Gerard, *The Europe Report: a Win/Win situation*, Mayor of London/Greater London Authority, August 2013
[113] Schwab, Klaus et al ,*The Global Competitiveness Report 2013-14*, WEF, Geneva, 2013
[114] Becker, Why small has become beautiful, *Becker-Posner Blog, www.becker-posner-blog.com,* sourced on 24 July 2014.

and the general reduction in trade barriers. It is quite conceivable that another form of trading relationship with the EU, such as accepting EU regulations for exports but avoiding social legislation, could have brought not dissimilar or even greater benefits to the UK, given the pattern in any case for trade between rich geographically close economies to increase.[115]

Will the Single Market meet the challenges of the future?

We have analysed the purely economic issues concerning the EU trade bloc and the Single Market. Despite the anecdotes and complaints of the regulatory cost impact of Single Market it is not widely viewed that the burden would be much reduced if the UK were to leave the EU and it remains one of the most difficult trade –offs to assess. However, an extensive study of the impact of regulation on economic growth in the US since 1949 reported that regulation reduced GDP by 2 % per annum[116] by slowing productivity growth. This indicates the importance of not overregulating and can be contrasted with the complaints concerning the Commission's incessant demand to legislate and the calls from the Netherlands and others to honour the principle of subsidiarity that have so far been ignored. Perhaps the lack of sympathy in the EU institutions is not surprising when we consider that in 2010, Mario Monti, in his review of the Single Market, restated that the EU was a compromise between different "varieties of capitalism "with a fuller embracing of competition by social market economies in return for some readiness to address social concerns through" targeted measures by Anglo Saxon orientated members".[117] This invariably means more employment related regulation and ignoring global pressures.

For some powerful UK actors, notably the CBI and social democratic parties, this remains a very acceptable compromise. Big business has the ability to lobby for its interests in Brussels and bear the costs of regulation and compliance, it can indeed produce barriers to competition in their interests. However, from a free market viewpoint more emphasis is devoted to factors such as the constraining of innovation and competition via harmonisation of product and labour standards. One example of this is the use of the "precautionary principle" by the EU in its approval of new products and technology which measures the risk of harm of new developments, but not the benefits, and has been utilised to block the cultivation of GM crops and the use of some pesticides. For example an insecticide called neonicotinoids was subjected to a temporary two year ban by the EU in 2013 on the basis of contested research and heavy lobbying by Friends of the Earth of the potential harm to honeybees. This was on the basis of very large doses and the scientific evidence that in normal amounts the insecticide was harmless to bees had been accepted by the US authorities. The UK opposed the ban, having requested further testing, and the resultant use of an older less effective insecticide products severely impacted the 2014 rape crop (and incidentally the flowers bees obtain pollen from), and an emergency change in UK approvals. [118] The broader point was made by the UK's Chief Scientific Adviser when he wrote that the excessive use of the precautionary principle had become a "stop sign to innovation". He also noted that Europe was an outlier in ignoring scientific evidence on the safety of GM crops and the precautionary principle had become politicised.[119] Another damning comment on the stifling impact on EU standards was made by technical engineering entrepreneur James Dyson who has commented that in his field big German companies dominated standard setting and energy reduction committees and "so we get the old guard and the

[115] Rich geographically close countries trade grows as they each produce the type of goods in demand from their neighbours. It takes decades for emerging economies to produce the type of branded sophisticated goods in demand in high and middle income economies.

[116] Dawson & Seater, Federal Regulation and Aggregate Economic Growth in *Journal of Economic Growth,* January 2013

[117] Monti, *A strategy for the Single Market,* European Commission, 2010.

[118] Ridley, Matt, "A precautionary ban has made things worse for bees", in *The Times* , 13 October 2013

[119] Webster, Ben & Devlin, Hannah, "Safety-first rulings stifling innovation", in *The Times* 20 November 2014

old technology supported and not the new technology".[120] This reinforces our previous examination of trade agreements where the areas of negotiation have moved on from protecting national producer interests directly via tariffs, to protection achieved by regulation to protect consumers or to reflect the "values" of citizens, as often powerfully articulated by Green NGO's.

For the UK's future we need to consider if the institutions of the EU are appropriate and flexible enough to face the challenges and opportunities of the digital economy and globalisation, especially as the proportionate importance of the EU in global trade and global GDP will continue to fall. A completion of the Single Market in services would be beneficial to the UK, but we must question if economies suffering from the euro crisis are prepared to open up their markets further and undertake the necessary structural reforms. Moreover more integration invariably involves more regulation. In the words of Nigel Wilson (CEO of Legal and General), speaking of the service economy, "are the costs of trying to unify 28 countries prohibitively high? Everyone wants more trade but if it means more regulation, is it worth it?".[121] As discussed, regulation often protects incumbents and hinders the disruptive innovation that is an important factor in economic growth that the EU and the UK needs. In the EU, politicisation can hold back regulatory approvals for years if not decades. At a minimum this suggests that applying the principle of subsidiarity and delegating much more regulation to the national level together with exempting small companies from some matters is a necessary and important EU reform. From this cautionary Single Market overview we will now analyse some key Single Market impacts of the EU on the UK and their implications for the UK's future.

---

[120] Dyson, James, Interview on BBC *"Today"* programme, 21 November 2014.
[121] Wilson, Nigel, "One sided debate on Europe could force unnecessary Brexit", in *The Daily Telegraph*, 29 November 2014

The EU's Energy and Climate Change policy

The Policy and its impact

In 2007 the Lisbon Treaty expressed the objective of combating climate change. The general consensus in evidence presented to the UK governments competency review in 2014, was that EU initiatives had led to generally higher environmental standards, albeit with the general concerns about costs and regulation. However, the 2009 Climate Change and Regulatory Energy Package (CARE) introduced a group of measures which are among the most far reaching and costly measures ever undertaken by the EU. It ranged from the ban of old style light bulbs and the introduction of smart meters, energy efficiency labels and building regulations to some ambitious and major Co2 reduction initiatives for energy generation and industrial energy usage. We will discuss below some of the key energy policies and their impact, but it must be set within the context of the UK governments own enthusiasm to be a leader in environmental policy and the 2008 Climate Change Act's own ambitious targets to reduce Co2 emissions by 80% by 2050. This was passed by Westminster with virtually no dissent at the time. Cynically, this all party enthusiasm was probably an important forward indicator of the policy problems that have since arisen, but the European context has made the issues appreciably worse through locking in the inflexible and ultimately misguided measures introduced and the EU's wish to use the environmental agenda to demonstrate its "soft power". The UK can be viewed as a recent convert to the green agenda with the German Green party playing a role in government since the 1990's and the "Energiewende" (energy change) policy on renewables in Germany dating from 2000. The German sponsorship has clearly been a key factor behind the powerful EU measures.

While the UK has escaped the direct impact of the Euro, many of the CARE measures reflect the same EU policy culture of a rule based system and imposition, with insufficient attention to differences in individual nation energy networks and political hubris acting as a justification. The 2008 policy was based on the assumptions that fossil fuel prices were bound to rise; that Europe could build a competitive advantage by being a leader in renewable energy and could ameliorate the initial costs via a global deal; and that a carbon tax would encourage substitution by industry. All these premises have proven to be wrong and in 2015 the policy is fragmenting.[122]

In order to understand the impact of EU energy policy we will set out below what the Directive required and what some of the key outcomes have been.

The Directive required :

- The EU should source 20% of its overall energy from renewables by 2020. For the UK it meant 15% of total energy (ie. not just energy generation) from renewables by 2020 against a level of 1.3% in 2005, [123]the most ambitious target in the EU.
- 10% of transport fuels should be from biofuels.
- A central EU target for Co2 emission reduction utilising the Emissions Trading Scheme (ETS). Firms covered by the scheme (40% of total emissions), would be required to make a 21% cut in their emissions. Member states to reduce emissions from the rest of the economy on average by 10%.

The result for the UK has been:

---

[122] Butler, Nick, "European Energy Policy –time to start again", in the *Financial Times,* 27 October 2014
[123] Sir David King , Chief UK scientific adviser in 2008 opined that he thought it was a mistake and that Blair thought it meant energy generation

- It has been locked into an inflexible and expensive way of reducing Co2. Because of the short time frame to achieve an ambitious outcome it has forced a costly push into certain technologies (Wind, Solar), when there are a lot of uncertainties as to what alternative technologies will be best in the long run. Moreover large subsidies have been required to encourage investment. The reliance on an intermediate objective rather than focusing on reducing Co2 has prevented lower cost strategies such as gas substitution for coal generation (as in the US). The target is now viewed as completely unrealistic and in 2014 was negotiated away by the UK. On reflection it is difficult to see how the established renewable technologies could ever have expanded sufficiently to meet the UK's objectives, especially given the lack of expansion of renewable energy (including biofuel) utilisation in transport or heating.

- At the same time, under the 2001 Large Combustion Plant Directive, the UK has to close 25% of its generation capacity by 2020 relating to coal. The renewables focus has exacerbated the problem by reducing flexible generation capacity and raised the prospect of energy shortages.

- Subsequent concerns that some biofuel additives are harmful and can raise food prices has caused complications. It has proven to be unattainable and, again, its status as a necessary target in itself unhelpful.

- The ETS scheme has proved to have many flaws and unfit for purpose with various exemptions granted (particularly to help Eastern Europe) and combined, with the recession, the price of permits collapsed from €30 to under €5 in 2014. This has had an adverse effect on Co2 reduction with industry doubting even low cost low carbon alternatives worthwhile if permits have such little value. The UK indeed decided to put a floor on the ETS carbon price via a carbon tax.

- The impact on prices of EU regulations and targets raised the average household dual fuel bill by 5% in 2013 rising to 11% by 2020. For medium sized firms it is 9% in 2013 rising to 23% in 2020.[124] As there is no Single Market in energy prices, the UK's prices remain among the top quartile in the EU, despite a low tax take compared with many nations.

From an overall EU perspective, other global blocs have not responded by equivalent Green measures. The 2009 Copenhagen talks failed and the EU was "marginalised".[125] Moreover, attempting to use as a tool of soft power has blurred the environmental objective and caused difficulties, an attempt to introduce a carbon tax on foreign airlines angered the US, India, China and Russia.[126]

The misjudgement that the EU measures would be joined by other major countries with equivalent measures has been a significant negative factor for the UK and EU economy, leading to energy intensive industries offshoring and reducing other industries cost competitiveness. A medium sized industrial company in the EU now pays 20% more for its energy than China, 65% more than India and more than double than in the US.[127] This is also partially because the EU view of the dynamics of the energy market has proven to be completely wrong due to shale gas and cheap coal.

---

[124] Howarth, Christopher & Ruparel, Raoul, *Rotten Foundations: Time to reassess the EU's Environment and Climate Change Policies,* Open Europe, London, September 2014

[125] House of Lords European Union Committee, 7th report of session 2009-10

[126] BBC, Countries rally against EU carbon tax on airlines, www.bbc.co.uk/news/world-europe, 21 February 2012, sourced on 14 August 2015.

[127] Elliot, Matthew & Lewis Oliver, *Energy Policy and the EU,* Business for Britain, London, 2014

Where now for EU Energy Policy?

In 2014 the EU set a new target of reducing CO_2 emissions by 40% by 2030 in a difficult negotiation with resistance particularly from Eastern European nations, which will receive compensation payments. Criticised as too low by Greenpeace who lobbied for 55%, it was agreed as a basis for the 2015 global conference in Paris. Most importantly, the renewable energy target of 27% for 2030 is not binding on individual nations with this concession led by the UK and Poland. The differing national positions on fracking has also been recognised with regulatory decisions on if to pursue confirmed to be decided at the national level. This latter point is an example of a EU delegation to nations that the UK will hope to expand on in its renegotiations.

The EU now intends to devote its major efforts to improving energy market integration and building a common power market. As previously discussed this would be a good mechanism for the EU to use its bloc advantage, by enabling the sharing of energy resources and improving energy security. At present some 30% of EU gas imports come from Russia, (five EU countries exclusively rely on Russian gas), while the large Spanish wind energy resources, for example, are trapped by poor connections with the French grid. Rapid progress is extremely unlikely, however, as the capital expenditure required to integrate electricity networks is huge and large differences in domestic customer energy tariffs, (due to different levels of national taxation), confirm the lack of a single market. The Eastern European nation's focus on cost and energy security is causing frictions and enabling Russia to use gas as a means of dividing the EU. More positively, the Commission aims to sanction Gazprom for abusing its market dominance in overcharging countries with limited other supply options and for restricting others from reselling gas. With the EU a major energy importer, energy is thus a strategically key foreign policy issue for the EU going forward including efforts to diversify away from Russian gas.

For the UK, the top down EU measures avoiding subsidiarity on execution, have been a very costly mistake in which the UK government and officials were enthusiastically complicit. As the UK exceeded the EU requirements, we cannot necessarily blame the EU for the outcome. UK government impact assessments indicate costs to the UK economy of over £20bn with few offsetting benefits materialising.[128] Moreover, many of the issues were identified at the time by critics such as Open Europe.[129] In particular, policy ignored the cheaper alternatives to reducing CO_2 in its focus on subsidised renewables and confirms again the downsides of inflexible rule based systems which cannot be easily revised due to the EU processes. Energy security and grid integration initiatives by the EU are to be welcomed, but of course would be possible for the UK in a looser relationship. The UK has recently announced a major investment to improve grid linkage with Norway, for example, and is exploring links to Icelandic geothermal power.

---

[128] Open Europe, *Top 100 EU rules cost £33.3bn*, *www.openeurope.org.uk* , sourced 19 March 2015
[129] Open Europe*, The EU Climate Action and Renewable Energy Package: Are we about to be locked into the wrong policy?* London, 2008

The City and Financial Services.

The Facts: The UK has a 70% market share of financial services in the EU. 78% of all foreign exchange trades and 85% of hedge fund management occurs in the City. Financial services accounted for 7.9% of UK GDP in 2012.[130] In the 17 years to 2008 UK financial service exports grew at a compound rate of 12.8% and from 2008-13 by 2.2%. Total financial exports in 2013 were about £60bn or approximately 4% of GDP[131]. However export of financial services to non EU countries is twice the size of those to the EU. The City is a key employer for London which itself is the 9th largest economy in the EU.[132] The passport system of EU regulation applies to banking operations in the EU and has been an important factor in the City's dominance.

The financial services industry is a key strength of the UK and one that has been seriously weakened in recent years by the financial crisis. This has produced policy reactions to improve regulations and controls at the national, EU and global levels. A further issue has subsequently been the Euro crisis which has in turn led to banking supervision measures to move towards banking union in the Euro area. Three new EU institutions have been formed: The European Banking Authority domiciled in London, The European Insurance and Occupational Pensions Authority in Frankfurt and the European Securities Authority in Paris. This is moving the EU towards a common regulatory culture decided by QMV in the Council and with disputes settled by the ECJ. More worryingly for the UK, the new institutions working with the Commission are establishing powers that cannot be challenged.

In continental Europe and within the European Union institutions the Great Recession was initially viewed as a crisis arising in the banking system and of Anglo Saxon capitalism. The UK's dominance within Europe in finance has historically meant that the EU had not attempted to intervene in the management of the City, but the 2007 failure of Northern Rock and subsequent events undermined the UK's reputation. Combined with the EU's extended competencies arising from the Lisbon Treaty, the EU now has a very significant role in financial regulation. This is alarming due to the fact that some important actors appear intent to reduce the importance of the City with implications for the whole UK economy. For example a proposal for a Financial Transaction Tax by the European Commission has as one of its objectives to "create appropriate disincentives for certain transactions " and to reduce the volume of "derivatives and financial-bets" by 75%.[133] The UK is in the difficult position of requiring access to the Single Market while facing regulatory challenges that it is struggling to contain and in some cases outright hostility to its role. A recent poll of 408 City leaders found that 43% thought the EU was hostile to the City and only 16% that supported it.[134] The UK's own domestic politics are also hardly helpful to standing up to Brussels to protect bankers, for example Labour MEP's voted in favour of the Financial Transaction Tax and recently increased banking taxes has meant that institutions such as Standard Chartered and HSBC are reportedly considering relocating their headquarters to Asia. The EU is only one component of much heavier financial regulation.

The key challenges faced include a series of measures such as a financial transaction tax, emergency powers to ban short selling and restricting banker's bonuses, all which appeal to a European model

---

[130] TheCityUK. *Key facts about UK financial and professional services*, The CityUK, January 2014.

[131] Congdon, Tim, *The City of London in retreat,* Brugge Group, London, 2014

[132] see Lyons, 2014

[133] European Commission, *Implementing enhanced co-operation in the field of the Financial Transaction Tax* European Commission 23 January 2014. Some EU nations are attempting to use the enhanced co-operation process in the face of opposition by the UK which is currently undertaking asking the ECJ if the process can be used.

[134] Gordon, Sarah, "City Support for EU based on resignation not enthusiasm", in *the Financial Times*, 21 April 2015

of finance and the prejudices of populism, but are actually harmful to the financial markets. Transaction tax and short selling restrictions would have the impact of seriously reducing market liquidity and thus the proper functioning of markets[135] . Banking bonus restriction leads to higher base salaries and thus reduces the cost flexibility of institutions, a point made by Mark Carney, the Governor of the Bank of England.[136] These matters are currently being fought by the UK, primarily through the ECJ, but without success to date. An ECJ ruling to affirm the short selling arrangements and dismiss the UK's argument that the ESA did not have authority, unusually overturned the ECJ's Attorney General's support of the UK's case. This defeat for the UK was viewed as a political assertion by the ECJ of the powers of the new regulatory institutions.

The UK established some protection to its rights by ensuring a level playing field throughout the EU for banking regulation via a "double lock" for EBA decisions of requiring a majority of both Euro and non Euro members. Even so the environment remains largely unsupportive. Hedge funds and private equity, symbolic of Anglo Saxon capitalism and mostly based in London have been subject to restrictions viewed as disproportionate. Solvency II regulations for insurance companies have involved heavy costs for the important UK international insurance market, but delays caused by French and German insurers has meant the "mounting costs" were, in the words of a senior Bank of England Official "frankly indefensible".[137] Some international insurers have relocated to the Bahamas.

The appointment of the UK's Lord Hill as the Financial Services Commissioner in October 2014 was seen as a victory for the UK and recognition, perhaps, that the UK's key industry needs a strong voice in Brussels. It is also a recognition in Brussels of the requirement to develop new methods and instruments of credit in Europe and the dominant role that London would play in the development of leasing, securitisation and Equity IPO markets. This reflects the fact that unlike the US, bank intermediation has dominated the provision of credit in Europe with bank balance sheets four times larger than EU GDP, compared with 0.8 of GDP for the US[138]. The problems of the dominant and damaged banking industry means that the EU economy is suffering from low credit growth which has constrained recovery and requires new intermediaries to transmit credit. In the US only 30% of investment is financed by banks compared with 70% in Europe.[139]"Capital Markets Union" is viewed by the new Commission as one of its key initiatives to improve economic performance by providing new channels to put European savings to better use, make the channels more diverse and thus more resilient and encourage more equity raising to improve risk sharing and investment options for European pension funds. The City clearly has a potentially major role to play.[140]

In summary the City shows many aspects of the conflicts and paradoxes of the EU including:

- The City has benefited greatly from the Single Market. In 2013, 249 of the 352 banks located in London were foreign owned and the City of London Corporation noted that they invested in London because of access via the EU passport for financial services.[141]It also explains why Swiss Banks have major UK incorporated subsidiaries. The development of a unified Euro capital market has been particularly beneficial. Moreover there is future strong potential and the EU needs London's expertise.

---

[135] The Transaction Tax concept has run into difficulties with a pilot scheme by France failing to raise significant revenues due to low transaction volumes.

[136] Carney, Mark, "EU bonus cap has unfortunate side effects", in *CityAM*, 17 January 2014

[137] Congdon, p29.

[138] Dixon, "*The* EU *needs a modern* financial *system*" in *Financial Times*, 14th July 2014.

[139] Stated by Lord Green at City of London/Open Europe Conference on 20 January 2015

[140] Points made by Sir Jon Cunliffe, Deputy Governor of the Bank of England at City of London/Open Europe Conference on 20 January 2015.

[141] All Party Parliamentary Group for European Reform, *Inquiry into the EU single market in services*, 2013, p. 16

- Regulation is an overbearing concern and one where the UK is struggling to protect the City's interests against actors that can be anti-financial markets and Anglo Saxon capitalism. The City's trade surplus is approximately two thirds dependent on trading outside the EU, but some potential regulations for deepening the internal market will make this more difficult and potentially harm London's status as a global financial centre. Indeed a 2014 survey found that the double impact of UK and EU regulations was leading to 64% of financial service participants considering operating elsewhere. In the words of the survey "The UK financial services market does not believe it has control over its own regulation".[142]The City is generally fearful of the uncertainty of leaving the EU, but wishes the UK managed the issues more effectively. It is not difficult to imagine that France or Germany are more effective in protecting their own strategic economic interests.

The infrastructure of the City including buildings, intellectual capital, the adaptability of English common law, support services such as law and consultancy, dominates the European financial market industry. There are more banks represented in Edinburgh than Frankfurt and the practicality of any rapid relocation can be questioned, especially given London's global orientation. An econometric review of the positives and negatives led the Mayor of London, in his 2014 report, to suggest that London and the UK would be best served to remain in a reformed EU, but better to form a new relationship with the EU than remain in an unreformed bloc.[143]

Events concerning the Euro are likely to play an important role in any future decision as the Euro area forms its own institutions to police banking union and a single supervisory mechanism. A more integrated Euro area is unlikely to be happy to have London acting as its main financial centre, which is creating a battle ground over the primacy of the regulatory requirements of the Euro area versus the Single Market legislation for the whole EU. The "double majority lock" voting rules in the EBA provide some protection, but with smaller members due to eventually join the euro, this may eventually be lost. In March 2015 the UK won a significant case at the ECJ when the ECB's attempt to force security and derivative clearing houses for euro denominated instruments to be located in the Eurozone to ensure liquidity in a crisis, was overturned on the basis of its action being outside the ECB's competence. It subsequently appears that the ECB has accepted defeat, but it is unclear if this signals a general change in attitude to the City. This means financial regulation will be an important battleground in the renegotiation.

The economic bargain of the EU- a Conclusion on the Single Market

As previously discussed UK membership of the EU has normally been addressed as an economic decision. The business interests that are alarmed by the possibility of Brexit avoid discussing issues of sovereignty. In this section we have focussed on the economic results of the Single Market and have been unable to identify significant advantages in favour of the original decision for joining the EU rather than another type of free trade arrangement. Moreover through regulation, social measures and energy costs the EU imposes economic costs. These costs have been incurred while in many areas important to the UK, the Single Market is far from operational. The Asian economies and NAFTA have both grown their intraregional and external trade without much of the baggage associated with the Single Market. Switzerland exports four and a half times more to the EU per capita from outside that the UK does from within.[144] Joining did not "save" the UK economy as the original proponents of joining implied, it was the economic reforms of the 1980's and 1990's which

[142] BDO, *Friends or Foe:From conflict to collaboration in UK Financial services,* London, 2014.
[143] Lyons
[144] European Commission, *Trade Policy: Switzerland,* (2014)

was the crucial factor. Similarly Germany in the 1990's was seen as the new sick man of Europe with GDP growth averaging only 1.2% pa between 1991-2005. Its own reforms led to its revival while the wider EU sponsored agenda set out originally at Lisbon 2000 have been a conspicuous failure.

The EU economic growth model has not worked and an increasing divide has opened up between the growth led northern economies and the Mediterranean cluster of which France has become a member. Free market reforms, encouraged also by the ECB as part of the solution to the uncompetiveness arising from the Euro, is resisted in those nations. We have seen that the institutions of the EU do not encourage the innovation or productivity growth required for economic growth, while some 40% of its budget is spent on CAP.

The City stands out as a beneficiary of the Single Market, but again the UK's natural advantages in this area would have still led to its expansion, perhaps as an offshore centre. In the 1960's and 1970's it was US regulations which had led to the offshore Eurodollar market in London and an important phase of the City's expansion. The City's future could again be as an offshore financial centre, this time serving Europe as well as other international markets which in total are twice as important as the EU to the UK and growing faster. At this point in time protection of the interests of the City is a key issue, irrespective of any negotiations on the UK's future in the EU. On any future negotiations on Brexit, if the UK was outside the EU, it would become the EU's single largest export market accounting for 21% of its exports. This is an important counterweight in negotiations relating to the exports of the City to Europe, which the UK would seek to protect.

While the City has faced difficult times in recent years the UK "Digital economy", defined broadly, has expanded dramatically. For example the UK has the highest proportion of online retail in the world.[145] "Silicon Roundabout" in London now leads Silicon Valley in some fields of digital innovation and is the key centre in Europe. This indicates that the EU's efforts to create a European digital marketplace is likely to be an important factor in the future value of membership to the UK. However, it is already noted that an important factor in digital leadership has been the ability to attract talent from around Europe. London has become the European equivalent to California for many talented EU citizens in both the financial and digital economies, which is an issue we will discuss in the next section.

Open Europe estimates the politically realistic range of GDP outcomes arising from a Brexit in 2030 at only minus 0.8% to + 0.6%.[146] This supports our premise above that much of the regulatory burden would be likely to remain and also the limitations of the Single Market impact. It emphasises the point that UK specific characteristics (that for example is presently driving the expansion of the UK digital economy), rather than the EU is the dominant factor in economic performance. Of course, if the EU was to turn in on itself as a result of the euro crisis and protectionist instincts, then the bargain becomes less acceptable. However in those circumstances the UK would have north European allies for developing a new form of EU relationship.

Perhaps, therefore, the most pragmatic and sensible course would be to devote the energies that would be expended on negotiating Brexit to the reform of the EU. It is easier to negotiate from within than from the outside. It would minimise business uncertainty and benefit from the possibility that the economic fortunes of the Eurozone will improve if nations are forced into supply side reform.

---

[145] McWilliams, Douglas, *The Flat White Economy*, Duckworth, London, 2015 p. 172
[146] Booth et al, *"What if" The consequences, challenges and opportunities facing Britain outside the EU*, Open Europe, London, 2015

Immigration and Demographic Trends

The Facts: "Natural" population increase occurs when the birth rate is higher than the death rate. Overall population trends also depends on migration flows. The rate of increase in the EU population due to natural factors has declined and is expected to result in a declining EU natural population imminently. This is evidenced by in 1992 -2011, the EU 27 population increasing by 1.5 m per annum compared with 3.3m in the 1960's. In 2011 almost 75% of the EU population increase resulted from inward migration rather than a natural increase. The EU Total Fertility Rate (TFR) in 2012 was 1.6 births per woman compared with a sustainable rate of 2.1. A level below 1.5 is known as the "low fertility trap" where insufficient potential mothers over a few decades will mean the population can never recover, a current feature in some EU states including Poland, Spain, Germany and Italy. This is contributing to an ageing of the EU population with a median age of 41.5 in 2012 compared with 37.7 in 1992. On current trends with current inward migration levels of 1m pa, the EU old age dependency ratio (over 65's) will rise from 28% to 58% in 2060.

The diversity of the social and economic conditions in the EU produces very different population trends for both natural and migration factors with countries such as Spain and Italy facing a combination of low fertility, high emigration and an ageing workforce. Population growth in Germany and Italy is solely due to immigration and Germany has the smallest proportion of people in the 0-14 age bracket in the EU. Germany, France, the UK and Italy account for approximately 54% of total EU population, but while the UK and France have generally healthy natural trends the German TFR of 1.3, compared with 1.9 in the UK. Taking into account current migration flow levels, by 2050 the UK will be the largest country in the EU with a population of 72m versus a German population that will have reduced from 82m to 71m and a French population that is projected to increase from 62 to 68 million. In the UK in 2005 75% of population growth was accounted for by migration, but since then natural growth has benefited from a mini baby boom and is presently the current largest source of increase. Overall the UK's population increased by 14% to 64m in the period 1980-2013.

2010 figures indicate that some 2.2m UK citizens live elsewhere in the EU (400k retired) including 1m in Spain. This compared with 2.3m EU foreign nationals in the UK. In the year to June 2014 over 583k migrants arrived in the UK and 323k left giving a net inward migration of 260k of which 142k were from the EU, up from 106k in 2013. Net migration to the UK rose from 48k p.a in 1997 to 185k in 2003. Following the 2004 EU membership expansion inward migration rose and peaked at 320k in the year to June 2005. Historically non EU migration to the UK has been the most significant, accounting for some two thirds of the 4m net foreign migration 1997-2010. Government controls on non EU immigration is increasing the relative weight of EU immigration to a projected 50-60%. Almost all EU inward UK migration is work related and, in the past 10 years, EU migrants have left the UK at about half the rate at which they have arrived. Different patterns are exhibited by the relative wealth of nations, with migrants from poorer EU countries more likely to stay permanently and Romanian and Bulgarian migrants projected to account for approximately 40% of forecast long term net EU migration of 130k.[147]

The evolution of the EU has led to EU citizens having a general right of movement and residence, irrespective of economic activity and is underpinned by a broad set of rights to protect against

---

[147]Migration Watch, *EU Employment and Social Situation*, Quarterly Review, March 2013

Rigby, Elizabeth, "EU migrants moving to UK balanced by Britons living abroad" in the *Financial Times* 10 February 2014

Office for National Statistics, *Quarterly report*, November 2014

discrimination on the basis of nationality. For some, encouraging population movement was another means of breaking down nationalism EU members retain exclusive competence over the design of their social security systems, however the competence retention has been heavily ameliorated by the evolving rights of EU citizenship. The interpretation of rights has effectively restricted the UK's ability to differentiate between new arrivals and its own citizens. With the UK unusual in most working age benefits based on residence rather than an insurance based contribution record, this can produce a number of issues where the UK Government hopes to obtain concessions on in its renegotiations.

The 2004 enlargement and the subsequent economic crisis radically changed the landscape of EU labour mobility, as it created a large new pool of labour in economically poorer nations with unrestricted access to the UK. As previously noted, the UK was one of only three nations (Sweden and Ireland were the others), that did not impose the available transitional restrictions on the "EU 8 "from central and eastern Europe. This led to a major increase in EU immigration. Official estimates puts the increase in EU nationals resident in the UK over the period 2004-12 at 1.2m to a total of 2.3m with 700k Polish nationals now the second biggest single group of all foreign nationals.[148] A 2015 study by the Migration Observatory at Oxford University has estimated that in the period 2011-14 England's population rose by 565,000 due to migration. The continued weak economic conditions in Europe and tightened rules for non EU countries, meant that two thirds were from the EU.[149] Thus the issue of immigration and EU membership will remain closely linked.

The evidence of the overall economic impact of the new EU migration is inconclusive. In the UK Government's Balance of Competencies Review, a variety of evidence was quoted. For example the National Farmers Union reported "It has alleviated skills shortages and provided a welcome source of energetic and motivated workers eager to undertake work that is not been filled by the resident labour force".[150] Certainly, to the detriment of their home nations, the most motivated and talented are likely to be attracted to better opportunities in the UK and at all levels of the employment market, employers rely on immigration from both inside and outside the EU to meet their labour requirements. In the UK it can be argued that the ability to suck in large amounts of new labour disguised the "boom" in the UK economy up to 2008 as otherwise excessive wage inflation due to labour shortage would have been evident.

The drawbacks of large inward migration are best summarised by Open Europe in its evidence to the Competency Review:

"The free movement of workers within the EU has the potential to boost growth and competitiveness in both the UK and Europe…..However, free movement throws up a number of huge challenges, such as substantial loss of national control over who can enter the country, increased competition in low skilled sectors of the labour market, downward pressure on wages, and increased demands for public services and infrastructure"[151]

One can add that the plentiful supply of immigrant labour combined with the UK's labour law flexibility has discouraged wage growth and capital investment and thus contributed to the UK's low productivity growth.

The pressures or perceived pressures of EU migration has indeed produced a sea change in the UK's attitude with YouGov polling in September 2013 indicating that free movement was opposed by a

[148] HM Government, *Review of the Balance of Competencies :Single Market: Free Movement of Persons*, 2014, p. 27

[149] Migration Observatory, *Major new analysis of regional migrant populations of England*, www.migrationobservatory.ox.ac.uk, 6 March 2015, sourced 10 August 2015.

[150] HM Government, *Review of the Balance of Competencies :Single Market: Free Movement of Persons*, p31

[151] HM Government, *Review of the Balance of Competencies, Single Market: Free Movement of Persons*, p26

margin of 49% to 38% versus two-to-one in favour in 2005. It is another irony of the UK's relationship with the EU that the Labour party's ideological pre disposition to playing down the impact of immigration and Blair's enthusiasm to lead from the front on the expansion of the EU into central and eastern Europe, is behind much of the current uncertainties as to the UK's future relationship.

The recent rise of immigration to the top of the UK- EU agenda is evidenced by the fact that David Cameron's landmark 2013 Bloomberg speech did not even mention immigration as a problem. With the growth of UKIP and its success in the 2014 European elections, a political consensus appears to have been rapidly established among the other major political parties in the UK that, at a minimum, measures should be taken to reduce the availability of in-work benefits and tax credits to EU migrants. This recognises the social security systems role in boosting income and distorting the labour market, by making UK employment more attractive than pure wage rates would dictate. At present a single worker on the minimum wage in the UK would be able to earn four and a half times what they could earn in Romania including housing benefit and working tax credit. For a worker with a dependent spouse and two children it is almost nine fold more with income of over £28,000, 66% paid for by the tax payer.[152]

Proposals to avoid paying such benefit payments to immigrants for a number of years, and which do not require EU treaty change, were developed by Open Europe and are driving the agenda.[153] It seems likely that their adoption (which appears to have the support of Chancellor Merkel), could be significant in reducing the flow of low wage migrants, but are unlikely to satisfy the most strident critics. The Brussels narrative on freedom of movement is also moving in the UK's direction, partially due to illegal immigration and asylum seekers and possibly Islamic extremists from North Africa and other neighbouring countries, such as Kosovo, entering the EU. It is a major foreign policy issue for the EU to find ways to face the challenge of the poor, rapidly growing and often unstable nations on its southern borders. Bordering countries such as Italy and Greece are under EU law responsible for their management and welfare, but there is plenty of evidence that due to the Schengen agreement, they are able to leave and travel to the more accommodating northern Europe. The UK's position is thus bolstered further by calls by others to row back on unrestricted border movement. Five EU countries the UK, Germany, Italy, Sweden and France take 75% of inward EU asylum seekers which is leading to calls to share the burden more equally in Europe.[154]

Labour mobility is one strand of globalisation and greater connectivity which seems impossible to reverse on present trends and is a feature of all open economies. Of course if the UK left the EU it could introduce an Australian style points system for EU immigration, but then UK citizens could face reciprocal difficulties living and working in the EU. Moreover, as we shall discuss below, it is healthier to be a recipient of migratory flows and population increases than face the difficulties of a reducing population. Thus while recognising the strains on public services and infrastructure of the UK's rising population and the cultural and social impacts, this must be balanced by the economic benefits. The UK's dramatically better demographic trends, assisted by inward migration from the EU have the following advantages compared with Germany, Italy and Spain, and others:

---

[152] Migration Watch, *The Outlook for EU Migration : Migration Watch Briefing Paper 4.29,* 2014, www.migrationwatchuk.com/briefing-paper/4.29, sourced on 15 January 2015.

[153] Chalmers & Booth, *A European labour market with national welfare systems,* Open Europe, *2014.*

[154] Quoted by Stephen Meyer, German MP and Chair of German British Parliamentary Group at Open Europe conference on 12 March 2015.

- With a growing population the UK can ameliorate the increase in the age dependency ratio, i.e. the predicted fall in the number of economic active citizens supporting the aged (who are also benefiting from longer life expectancy). UK public finances will be less strained that in other countries with a higher dependency ratio.
- Population growth drives economic growth. A larger workforce and domestic market increases national income and makes the UK a relatively larger national economy.

In a world where many economies are or will be facing substantial challenges from population decline, the UK's position should mean that it will become the largest economy in Europe and retain its position as one of the largest economies in the world. A 2010 HSBC study "The World in 2050 " analysed current trends and confirmed the loss in relative size of many European economies, but maintains the UK as the sixth largest economy in the world.[155] This beneficial position for the UK was confirmed in January 2015 by the McKinsey Global Institute which analysed how much economic productivity must increase to compensate for the decline in the working population. It calculated that if productivity improvements remained at the same very high level as in the past 50 years, the fall in population would still mean that potential growth in the size of most economies will fall dramatically. On current population trends, the potential growth rate of Germany falls 52%, Italy 36%, France 18% and the UK only 10%, compared with growth in 2007-12![156] [157]

There are three conclusions we can reach from this analysis of the future paths of European economies. Firstly, the UK is likely to be in an increasingly powerful position economically. This can either improve its leverage in discussions with the EU or provide some confidence that the UK is not becoming an economic minnow in world terms and could realistically change its relationship with the EU. Secondly, it confirms the decline in the relative size of the EU economy and the requirement to be outward looking and to continue to embrace globalisation. Finally, the lack of population growth reinforces the importance of productivity improvements and innovation to raise national income. This again leads us back to the question as to whether the institutions and practices of the EU are an effective framework for encouraging necessary innovation and providing the incentives for the productivity improvements that are required to raise national incomes.

THE EU AND UK FOREIGN POLICY

A review of the foreign policy challenges facing the UK and EU in 2015 is daunting. Moreover these challenges are occurring in a world where the secular trend of greater and greater global interdependence is occurring alongside a decline in the geopolitical power of the US and the West generally. In the words of Ian Bremmer, we are in the "G-Zero " world where, although the US retains substantial economic and military leadership, "there are a growing number of emerging powers that cannot change the global status quo, but they can ignore what the US wants and even block US plans they don't like".[158] Others such as Gideon Rachman point to the falling confidence in the superiority of the West's democratic and free market model in the light of failed military interventions, the banking crisis and a largely malfunctioning US political system.[159]

---

[155] Wood, Karen, *The World in 2050,* HSBC Global research, London, January, 2012
[156] It should be noted that this is measuring the total size of each economy rather than the per capita GDP position(ie income per person –a standard of living measure), which again falls in the projections, but by a smaller amount.
[157] McKinsey Global Institute, *Global Growth, can productivity save the day in an ageing world?* 2015.
[158] Bremmer, "America's Uneasy Path abroad", in *Time Magazine,* 18 December 2014
[159] Rachman, Gideon, "The West has lost its intellectual self confidence", in the *Financial Times,* 6 January 2015

For the EU with its requirement for consensus among 28 member states and a faltering economic performance, its power and influence is subject to even greater challenge. Moreover events first in Libya and then in Ukraine, combined with a spat over surveillance also points to the looser relationship between Europe and the US, probably to the detriment of Europe's global influence. The EU's failure to deal with the euro crisis has not impressed the US administration. Tim Geithner, former US Treasury Secretary in interviews for his memoirs recalled, "I completely underweighted the possibility that they would flail around for three years. I thought it was just unconceivable to me that they would let it get as bad as they ultimately did."[160]

Chapter 2 outlines the history of the EU's foreign policy activities and we can point to some successes relating to trade sanctions, civilian crisis management, the promotion of human rights and coordinating nuclear discussions with Iran. The reality is, however, that the UK, France and Germany all have different aspirations and philosophies for foreign policy with Germany remaining to date largely pacifist, the French wishing to develop the EU military organisation , while the UK focuses on NATO as the appropriate vehicle. Moreover unified or QMV can lead to "lowest common denominator" results and the institutional tensions within the EU (for example between the Commission and the EEAS or the Council and the Parliament), impedes effectiveness. Most recently Russia has been looking to exploit the different interests between Eastern and Central European members and the remainder, while the new Greek government is exhibiting pro Russian sentiments. The other growing challenge are the migration and terrorist threats from the EU's southern borders, some 400 million people that are poor and expanding in number rapidly. This also requires coordinated European attention.

In this environment the UK has viewed the EU as one of its portfolio of options, useful in some circumstances but not in others. This reflects not only the practical limitations on the EU's capabilities but the Foreign Office wisely wishing to guard against the creeping EU competence of the "methode Monnet" and its diplomatic officials, whose new loyalties are encouraged by very generous remuneration, well in excess of their nation state peers. Thus, in the Review of the Balance of Competencies relating to Foreign Policy, the point is made that EU officials when discussing areas of shared competence must state that it is delivered also on behalf of the member state to guard against the Commission or the EEAS claiming that "having represented the Member States on an issue, it has gained unfettered competence to act".[161]To the irritation of some, the UK, rather than fully embracing the EEAS, has also increased its cooperation with Commonwealth countries with some co location of overseas missions. On the other hand reduced resources in EU nation embassy's as a result of the EEAS has diminished the FO's capabilities both in putting the UK's case in some member states and a full analytical understanding of issues such as Russia.

It is in the area of Trade (excluding sanctions) and Energy policy, areas led by the Commission and governed by QMV, where the EU has proven to be most effective as a bloc. As previously discussed, standard setting, much to the annoyance of the Chinese, protects European commercial privileges by forcing others to take on the extra costs of meeting Western specifications. US and European companies are also able to charge licencing fees for the resultant use of IP. According to Ian Bremmer, this is likely to be a future battleground for the West as China in particular looks to push its own standards for high tech products in areas such as 4G products.[162] Both the EU and US negotiators for the Transatlantic Trade and Investment Partnership have also made the point that the Partnership will enhance the two bloc's joint negotiating position on such matters. At Davos in 2015, the US negotiator Michael Froman added that TTIP would display shared liberal values "when there are a lot of alternative models out there" and provide a bulwark to Europe in the face of

---

[160] Spiegel, Peter, "Draghi's ECB Management: the leaked Geithner files" in the *Financial Times,* 11 November 2014

[161] HM Government, *Review of the Balance of Competences, Foreign Policy,* 2013, section 3.35.

[162] Bremmer, Ian, *Every Nation for itself,* Penguin, London, 2013, p. 86

Russia's resurgence.[163]The risk for the EU is that if it fails to agree TTIP then it will further encourage the US to look to Asia in matters such as trade standards.

Of course many of the soft power advantages of the EU can be obtained by a looser arrangement (indeed TTIP will include Norway and other non EU EEA members), but the UK Foreign Office is consistently enthusiastic for the current arrangements. They also point to the importance to the UK-US relationship of the UK remaining a very significant vehicle of influence in EU, especially as US foreign policy priorities have moved to Asia. By looking to largely "exit Europe", the US has actually made the UK's task of influencing the EU agenda more difficult with recent events in Ukraine indicating that Europe has been severally weakened by US disengagement. With Putin aiming to weaken and disrupt the EU in any way he can including increasing his influence in the Balkan's, the possibility of the UK further damaging the EU by withdrawing could be very damaging to the UK-US relationship.

The diplomatic elite in the UK seem both disappointed by the failure of the EU to become now or in the foreseeable future a strong foreign policy actor and the UK's overall diminished role as evidenced by the Ukrainian crisis.[164]But perhaps they should look wider at the diminished position of the West and its supranational institutions, the Chinese Development Bank is now bigger than the World Bank for example. In these circumstances the UK appears wise to devote some of its energies in deepening its bilateral ties with the Commonwealth, which became a new emphasis under William Hague.[165] This policy is also tacit recognition of the integration of the world and the loss of power of the EU bloc. It is also the case that the enhanced role of National Security Agencies in the government's foreign policy strategy and execution also puts emphasis on the UK's security agency relationships with France and the "Five Eyes" group and away from the EU.

It was previously noted that by endorsing deeper economic integration in the Euro area the UK is endorsing a closer relationship among other of its neighbours that it will not participate in, a new foreign policy position. In these circumstances, retention of what influence it can retain in Europe arising from the UK's own economic size and world status, would support our continued engagement via EU membership in this uncertain world, alongside an independent global perspective. Given the UK's presently diminished international profile[166] it cannot afford to discount the EU as both a sizeable vehicle for its own international influence and to support an enduring interest to maximise the UK's influence in Europe. From the EU's viewpoint losing the UK would both diminish its power and authority practically and signify a major failure in the project. Both sides thus have a strong motivation to negotiate.

---

[163] Hill, Andrew et al, "Businesses rally support for transatlantic trade deal" in the *Financial Times* 23 January 2015

[164] Sir Brian Crowe and others remarked that the key communication channel was between Obama and Merkel in the Ukraine Crisis. Not mentioned was that she was the obvious choice and the other candidates were fully occupied with Middle East issues. It is also symptomatic of the lower diplomatic profile of the UK generally. – University of Buckingham seminar 14 January 2015

[165] In March 2015 the UK set a precedent by becoming the first G7 country to become a founding shareholder in the Chinese led Asian Infrastructure Investment Bank, reportedly to the irritation of the US , which reflects the UK's wish to widen its influence in Asia.It complements a planned major Chinese offshore banking centre in London.

[166] In the words of James Rubin at a Chatham House debate on 16.March 2015 the UK currently "barely enters the ring never mind punching above its weight ".

CONCLUSION

Veterans of the world wars founded the EU and moulded its philosophy of ever closer union. Today, supporters of the EU fight back against criticism by warning of the dangers to peace of a return to nationalism and complain that people have forgotten or become complacent about why Europe needs the EU. We would, however, conclude that the EU has overreached itself, but has managed to create an inescapable web, albeit one full of contradictions. The EU institutions have attempted to establish their own democratic mandate in competition with national democracies, but beneath the veil nations continue to promote their own national interests first, reflecting their own values and cultures. Moreover, the rise of populist parties in the European Parliament, presented as being a key vehicle for supranational democracy, is causing alarm as to what may follow in the 2019 elections and the implications for EU governance. If this is European democracy, it is not the type of democracy Brussels or those in power in its member states had in mind. Looking back, the 2005 rejection of the European constitution by referendums in France and the Netherlands provided proof of the enduring lack of affection for this rules based organisation. The democratic rejection, as others, was ignored because of Europe's claimed "destiny" and it has taken the euro crisis and the emerging migration crisis to bring to the front the predominance of national interests. It is these crises and their ramifications, rather than the UK, which is now blocking the road to further integration. Meanwhile, recently introduced EU rules on allergies require restaurants to undertake a detailed audit of all ingredients and a detailed disclosure of fourteen allergens in menus. So much for the claim that the EU is now concentrating on the big issues.

From the UK's perspective, she should have engaged in the formulation process in the early 1950's, which could have influenced the philosophy and institutional structure. Having missed that opportunity, the UK should have avoided membership and formed a looser arrangement. The EU did not rescue the UK economy, but at the time of entry her poor economic performance and declining power understandably meant it was an attractive route. Unfortunately most British politicians underestimated the attraction of integration to the other nations, perhaps because the UK's democratic culture is so different to how much of the Continent operates. History and the transience of borders has taught much of Europe to equate nationhood with war and bad government, compared with Britain's more benign experience. Our common law legal system and unwritten constitution, our institutions including the crown, all date back deep into the Middle Ages and there is nothing quite like it elsewhere in Europe. The differences in the democratic political culture is enduring. A Paxman style interview of Merkel is unimaginable, Brussels finds the UK press superficial and verging on the jingoistic in its treatment of European affairs. The Conservative party has committed the ultimate EU social gaff in calling for a referendum.

This paper has been unable to find evidence of any great economic benefits from membership compared with other trading arrangements that could have evolved and the EU has not been key to the UK's improved economic performance. The same issues of shared or restricted economic sovereignty would occur in any arrangement, but we could have avoided some of the downsides in social regulation and inflexible regulations in energy and some of the other aspects of sovereignty that the Norwegians and Swiss have been keen to retain. Most importantly in the service economy, so dominant in the UK economy, the Single Market is far from complete and despite enthusiastic calls for action, maybe never will be. This does not mean the EU has been bad for the UK economically, but it certainly has not been unequivocally a good thing with a complex maze of positive and negative factors. We should not presume that the UK's politicians and officials are any more enlightened or competent or less enthusiastic than the EU in passing rules and regulations, it is just that it is easier to hold them accountable and to reverse their mistakes. Indeed solving domestic policy failures such as housing and energy, would have a bigger positive impact for the UK then leaving the EU ever could. Keeping the UK out of the eurozone has been a crucial positive result, but it is difficult to categorise it as wise statesmanship, given Blair and the CBI would have taken the UK into the Euro if they could have. Maybe it is The Sun newspaper that saved the UK economy. What not joining the Euro inner core has meant, is that a reappraisal of the UK's position in Europe became inevitable.

Concerning immigration, we have made an economic case for remaining in the EU with the likely benefit of some welfare eligibility tightening, but should all concerns be subordinated to the economy? Nationhood requires a sense of identity and cohesion which is challenged by constant change. If avoiding the euro was a Blair era success, the failure to introduce transitional controls to eastern European migrants was a mistake with serious negative implications for the British working class. Three quarters of the 872,000 Eastern Europeans that have arrived since are in low skilled jobs and have depressed wages.[167] The danger for the main political parties is that the reform consensus they have formed on benefits reform for immigration is being "sold" to the electorate as a solution, when they all recognise it probably is not. Yet again the main parties are in danger of misleading the electorate over Europe. Of course there is a general populist concern about immigration in the EU which may enable a stricter policy to be achievable over the next few years. There is much talk of the sanctity of free movement, but if the Single Market in services is far from complete, why should population movement be so unrestricted?

The future at best lacklustre outlook for the economic performance of the eurozone, combined with unfavourable demographic trends means that Europe is increasingly removed from the engines of economic growth in Asia and America and the UK must likely look elsewhere for its growth drivers. Many in Europe recognise the economic challenges, but it is unclear if the necessary supply side reforms can be implemented, at least on the basis of EU initiatives. Economist are indeed concerned that the impact of enduring high unemployment is permanently reducing the economic potential of Europe. This means that the EU could in the future be a bigger drag on the UK's economic performance. This is particularly the case if EU regulation and the instincts of the European Parliament hinder innovation and flexibility and embrace protectionism. The UK has been much more economically successful than most in the EU in evolving, adapting and generating new employment and these characteristics must continue. The growth of the power of the European Parliament, against the UK's wishes, has been one of the major downsides to the EU's development; and is now a generally held nation state concern, especially as the Commission has become too close to Parliament.

You cannot put an economic number on the value of democratic accountability, however, in matters such as the extension in the range of "rights", it is surely the case that an ancient parliamentary democracy should retain its supreme authority. As discussed, the overbearing status of the 1972 European Communities Act is causing disquiet to Supreme Court judges as the EU has extended into the field of rights. It is the withdrawal of this type of federalism, driven by a wish to encourage a sentiment of EU nationhood in the eyes of its citizens that is likely to have the strongest British support and rightly so. But even with this basic call to patriotism and national sovereignty, the impact of leaving the EU maybe less than many consider. Global markets and institutions, the media and the ubiquitous digital dissemination of information and opinions, the judiciary, NGO's , multinationals, all work against sovereignty as exercised by the UK Government. Today, the execution of government is more complex, the civil service less well equipped and the large expansion in the use of judicial reviews (where interested parties can appeal to the courts against government decisions), which was hardly used 30 years ago, has meant it is difficult to get anything done. The EU is only part of the dispersal of power and leaving it would not be akin to waiving a

---

[167] Migration Watch, *The UK Labour Market-EU workers by occupational skill levels*, www.migrationwatchuk.com/briefing-paper/364, sourced 20 July 2015.

magic wand, especially with much EU legislation embedded in UK law and its status as our largest and closest trading partner.

The EU in turn is itself losing power to the conflicting trends of power fragmentation and the integration of the world. For example, it is caught in the middle between the trend for global standard setting in trade and the differing national attitudes to GM crops, fracking etc. Recognition of these forces indeed supports the UK's foreign policy of exploiting multiple means of exercising geopolitical influence, but it may also mean in the future that the EU ceases to be an effective vehicle for some trade negotiations. The outcome of the TTIP negotiations will be a key indicator.

The UK is a deeply Eurosceptic country and with the EU's major problems, the case is probably stronger than it has ever been to withdraw and form a new relationship with Europe. However, our review of current British attitudes to the EU illustrates the difficulty in following that course, as there is no clear consensus of what direction the UK would take outside the EU. Economically, free trade with the world, inward migration and deregulation would be the most beneficial, but would face serious opposition within Britain where, for example, the social impulse of the EU has much support. Moreover, entering a relationship similar to that held by Switzerland would still face the impact of many EU regulations, monetary contributions, and difficult issues concerning inward EU migration to be negotiated. We cannot either assume that exit negotiations would be conducted in a spirit of genial cooperation by the EU. The UK emerging as a large offshore competitor economy avoiding all the downsides of membership with its largest trading partner is not a likely scenario. We must also acknowledge the soft power benefit of the EU role in trade negotiations and its other foreign policy roles. In these matters EU withdrawal would amplify further the UK's diminished global importance, notably to its closest ally, the USA. Ultimately, however, international influence will largely flow from the UK's economic performance and global outlook in or out of the EU. Those who doubt it should ponder over how the UK's large defence budget is paid for and compare it with other defence budgets.

The UK cannot avoid that, for reasons of geopolitics and economics, its affairs are invariably tied to Europe and we have a clear strategic interest in its future. Indeed, the difficulties the EU faces are so severe that it is in the UK's national interest to be able to influence the EU responses to future crises from within. Our conclusion, therefore, is that the status quo is not acceptable and that the UK should attempt a significant renegotiation of membership before facing the alternative of exit and the uncertainty that would result. She should put as much effort into this process as it would ultimately have to put into an exit agreement. A renegotiation would also avoid both further challenge to the fragile UK union by Scottish nationalists and difficulties for Ireland.

The EU would be greatly damaged by the withdrawal of the UK, likely to become the EU's largest economy and currently its second largest budget contributor. It will be very incentivised to respond positively to renegotiation with British exceptionalism widely recognised. EU history has shown that when there is a political will there is a way, for example measures taken to protect the euro are illegal under EU law and require future treaty change. The motivation to be sympathetic applies especially to Germany and others in northern Europe, which share much of the UK's economic philosophy, while many nations share the wish to regain powers from Brussels. Helped by the weakness of the EU and the Conservative's election victory, the UK's negotiating position has never been stronger.

If the EU is capable of reform, particularly on the UK's timetable, of course remains to be seen. The European ideal is a religion which can defy logic and experience as clearly as the Scottish independence movement. It has a powerful bureaucracy subject to group think and false consciousness and with ego's and careers to protect. One is constantly struck how removed Brussels and many commentators can appear from the weak economic realities of much of the EU. Successful constitutions, as with the UK, must adapt to survive, but it may need a new generation of politicians and the peasant pitchforks of protest parties, post 2019, storming the gates, to produce radical European reform. In the meantime, a prospectus which approaches many of the issues not from an exclusive UK viewpoint would have the best chance of success.

In this endeavour the euro crisis can be helpful in two ways. Firstly, it requires a reengineering of institutions within the euro area to manage the closer co-operation they require and thus an opportunity to change arrangements for the non-euro countries. A multi-tier EU is a political fact. Secondly, the economic reforms in uncompetitive nations has and will require social and employment legislation reform at national level, consistent with subsidiarity and incidentally with the state level social policy delegation being followed in the USA .German ordoliberalism, each nation being primarily responsible for sorting out its own economic problems, is consistent with the UK agenda as are the pleas from the ECB for countries to embrace reform to encourage growth.

A UK wish list would include the following with Brexit to be pursued if they cannot be significantly achieved. It would help create a multi-dimensional rather than an integrationist EU and increase the power of national Parliaments.

- The end of "ever closer union" as the goal of nation states, or an opt out by the UK, which would in itself restrict the reach of the European Court of Justice.
- Utilisation and enhancement of existing "yellow card" and enhanced cooperation mechanisms, to allow groups of nations to avoid certain initiatives or cooperate on others and a "red card "for a group to repeal existing legislation. This would also protect non euro members from euro orientated measures.
- Essential national interest override of QMV to protect in the case of the UK, the City, modelled on the Luxembourg Compromise.
- The completion of the Single Market in services and the digital economy with appropriate sanctions for non-compliance.
- The application of subsidiarity and proportionality to regulations including the exemption of small businesses.
- A secure opt out to the Charter of Fundamental Rights which can be complemented by a UK Bill of Rights as proposed by the Conservative administration.
- Member states to determine their own mix of social and employment legislation in accordance with subsidiarity principles enabling the reduction of costly regulations (eg working times directive) and restrictions on welfare support for migrants, including UK tax credits.
- More focus on agreeing Free Trade Agreements and the completion of TTIP. If the EU is unsuccessful or unambitious in negotiations (and indeed in completing the Single Market in services), then the UK must secure a way of negotiating FTA's for trade in services.
- Reform energy policy to prevent offshoring of energy intensive industries.
- Reform of EU institutions to reduce costs and improve effectiveness including abolishing recycling of regional development funds to rich members.

The difficult negotiating balance in the proposals above is the different economic philosophies of member states that could hinder maintaining the advantages of supranationalism if more authority is returned to nations. To the UK's advantage, Europe is more capitalist and free market friendly thanks to the supranationalism of the Single Market, policed and enforced by the Commission. This, however, runs against the theme of a more national/intergovernmental governance suggested by some of the reforms above. Yet again, it indicates the complexity of the process but at least with the reforms suggested UK and like-minded partners can co-operate as minorities, for example on the single market service sector reform, without being held back by others.

More positively, the Juncker Commission priorities are Capital Markets Union and the Single Market in the digital economy and energy, all broadly good for the UK and which gives some grounds for optimism. In the case of the City, it has a crucial role in the economic stimulus of Capital Markets Union and so surely a solution can be found for different regulatory standards, particularly as the UK regime is in many cases tighter to guard against the risks of another financial crisis. However, the reform agenda over the next few years could be overtaken by events. When something cannot go on forever it stops, and that is the case with the current euro arrangements. In one scenario, Germany and others in Northern Europe could abandon the euro rather than accepting the full implications of monetary union.

It is clearly in Britain's interests to remain engaged in the hope that new institutional arrangements reflect the reality of the world in the 21st Century rather than the ideals of 60 years ago. Wherever events take the EU, we can only hope that British politicians and officials will be more successful and more transparent than their predecessors in negotiating the changes that will invariably occur over the next few years. Ultimately it may require, after a first negotiation, a crisis resulting from a close referendum result, to truly focus minds. Indeed as Jean Monnet said, "Europe will be forged in crises, and will be the sum of the solutions for those crises".[168]

---

[168] Monnet, Jean, *Memories,* quoted in a speech by Stanley Fisher, Federal Reserve Governor, May 2015, www.federalreservegov/newevents/speech, sourced 20 July 2015.

BIBLIOGRAPHY

All Party Parliamentary Group for European Reform, *Inquiry into the EU single market in services*, Open Europe, London, October 2013.

Aldrick, Philip, "Germany seems to have forgotten that rules are made to be broken" in *The Times* 29th November, 2014.

Barber, Tony, "EU Parliament's major parties vote together "in *Financial Times*, 11 March, 2015.

BBC, *"Countries rally against EU carbon tax on airlines "*, www.bbc.co.uk/news/world-europe-17114312, 21 February 2012, sourced on 14 August 2015.

BDO, *Friends or Foe:From Conflict to collaboration in UK Financial Services,* BDO Financial Research, London, December, 2014.

Becker, Barry, *"Why small has become beautiful"*, www.becker-posner-blog.com, sourced 24 July 2014.

Blair, Alasdair, *The European Union,* Oneworld Publications, London, 2012.

Best, Heinrich et al, *The Europe of Elites,* Oxford University Press, Oxford, 2012.

Boltho, Andrea & Eichengreen, Barry, *The Economic Impact of European Integration,* Centre for Economic Policy Research, London, 2008.

Bootle, Roger, *The Trouble with Europe,* Nicholas Brealey Publishing, London, 2014.

Booth, Stephen et al, *What if? The consequences, challenges and opportunities facing Britain outside the EU,* Open Europe, London, 2015.

Booth, Stephen & Howarth, Christopher, *The European Parliament: A failed experiment in pan-European democracy?* Open Europe, London, May, 2014.

Brady, Hugo, *Twelve things everyone should know about the European Court of Justice,* Centre for European Reform, London, 2014

Bremmer, Ian, *Every Nation for Itself,* Penguin, London, 2013.

Bremmer, Ian, "America's uneasy path abroad" in *Time Magazine,* 18 December, 2014.

Butler, Nick, " European energy policy-time to start again", in *Financial Times, 27* October 2014.

Cameron, David, Bloomberg speech, www.gov.uk/government/speeches/eu-speech-at-bloomberg, sourced on 13 August, 201

Carney, Mark, "EU bonus tax has unfortunate side effects" in *City AM,* 17 January 2014.

CBI, *Our Global Future*, London, November 2013

Camps, Miriam, *Britain and the European Community 1955-1963,* Princetown University Press, 1964.

Centre for European Reform, *The Economic Consequences of leaving the EU*, June 2014.

Chalmers, Damien & Booth, Stephen, *A European labour market with national welfare systems,* Open Europe, London, 2014.

Charter, David, *Europe: In or Out?,* Biteback Publishing, London, 2014.

Clifford Chance, *A legal assessment of the UK's relationship with the EU- A financial services perspective,* The CityUK, London, April 2014.

Congdon, Tim, *The City of London in retreat,* Brugge Group, London, 2014.

Cummings, Dominic, statement on working of government, www.dominiccummings.wordpress.com, sourced 7th August, 2014.

Dawson, John & Seater, John, "Federal Regulation and Aggregate Economic Growth" in *Journal of Economic Growth,* January, 2013.

Dempsey, Judy, statement on European Commission, www.carnegieeurope.eu, sourced 10 September, 2014.

Department of Business Innovation and Skills, *The economic consequences for the UK and the EU of completing the single market in services,* BIS economic paper no 11, February 2013.

D'Estaing, Giscard, "The EU Treaty is the same as the Constitution " in *The Independent,* 30 October 2007.

Dixon, Hugo, "The EU needs a modern financial system"in *Financial Times,* 14 July 2014

European Commission, *Proposal for a Council Directive implementing enhanced co operation in the field of the Financial Transaction Tax,* Document 520138PC0071, 2013.

European Commission, *Standard Eurobarometer 81,* Public Opinion Analysis Sector, Spring 2014.

European Commission, *Trade Policy: Switzerland,* 2014.

Europa-eu, statistics on EU budget, www.europa-eu, sourced 6 November, 2014.

Elliott, Mathew & Lewis, Oliver, *Energy Policy and the EU,* Business for Britain, London, 2014.

Evans-Pritchard, Ambrose, "Germany's record trade surplus is a bigger threat to the euro than Greece " in *Daily Telegraph,* 5 May, 2015.

Fresh Start Project. *The Single Market in Services,* www.eufreshstart.org, 2013.

Frost, David, *Gearing up for delivery: How to manage the negotiation,* Open Europe, 2015.

Fukuyama, Francis. *The Origins of Political Order,* Profile Books, London, 2011.

Giles, Chris & Parker, George, "Osborne Urges Eurozone to get a grip " in the *Financial Times,* 20 July, 2011.

Grant, Charles, *How to build a modern European Union,* Centre for European Reform, London, 2013.

Ganesh, Janan, *From a reluctant European: A memo to the PM,* Open Europe, London, 2015.

Gordon, Sarah, "City Support for EU based on resignation not enthusiasm " in the *Financial Times, 21 April 2015.*

Hill, Andrew et al, "Business rally support for transatlantic trade deal" in the *Financial Times,* 23 January, 2015.

HM Government, *Review of the Balance of Competences: Foreign Policy*, Foreign and Commonwealth Office, 2013.

HM Government, *Review of the Balance of Competencies: The Single Market,* Department for Business Innovation and Skills & the Foreign and Commonwealth Office, July 2013.

HM Government, *Review of the Balance of Competencies: The Single Market: Free Movement of Persons*, Home Office, July 2014.

HM Treasury, *The Economic Effects of EU membership for the UK*, 2005. https://www.gov.uk/government/uploads/system/uploads/attachment_data/file/220965/foi_eumembership_presentation.pdf

House of Commons, European Scrutiny Committee, twenty fourth report, *Reforming the European Scrutiny System in the House of Commons,* 2013-14 session, 20 November, 2013.

House of Commons, European Scrutiny Committee, forty third report, *The Application of the EU Charter of Fundamental Rights in the UK: a state of confusion, 2013-14 session,* 26 March, 2014.

House of Lords, European Union Committee, seventh report, *Stars and Dragons: The EU and China,* 2009 -10 session, 23 March, 2010.

House of Lords, European Union Committee, sixth report, *The EU and Russia: before and beyond* the *crisis in Ukraine,* 2014-15 session, 20 February, 2015.

Howarth, Christopher & Ruparel, Raoul, *Rotten Foundations, time to reassess the EU's environment and climate change policies,* Open Europe, London, September 2014.

Kelemen, R Daniel, footnotes 45, 46, *" Rorotoko"* http://rorotoko.com/interview/20110919_kelemen_daniel_on_eurolegalism_transformation_law_european_union/, 19 September, 2011.

Klein, Matthew, *"Michael Pettis explains the Euro crisis"*, www.ftalphaville.ft.com.

Lawson, Dominic, "Speaking for England" in *The Spectator,* 14 July, 1990.

Liddle, Roger, *The Europe Dilemma,* I.B. Tauris & Co, London, 2014.

Lindsell, Jonathan, *The Norwegian Way. A case study for Britain's future relationship with the EU,* Civitas, London, February, 2015.

Lyons, Gerard, *The Europe Report: A Win-Win situation,* Mayor of London/Greater London Authority, August, 2014.

McKinsey Global Institute, *Global Growth, can productivity save the day in an aging world?,* McKinsey and Company, 2015.

McWilliams, Douglas, *The Flat White economy,* Duckworth Overlook, London, 2015.

Meyer, Christopher, comments on Commission, https://twitter.com/SirSocks, sourced 25 October, 2014.

Migration Observatory, *Major new analysis of regional migrant populations of England,* http://migrationobservatory.ox.ac.uk/press-releases/major-new-analysis-regional-migrant-populations-england, 6 March 2015, sourced on 10 August 2015.

Migration Watch, *EU employment and social situation, Quarterly Review March 2013,* www.migrationwatchuk.com.

Migration Watch, *The outlook for EU migration: Migration watch briefing paper 4.29,* www.migrationwatchuk.com/briefing-paper/4.29, 2014.

Migration Watch, *The UK labour market-UK workers by occupational skill levels,* www.migrationwatchuk.com/briefing-paper/364, May 2015, sourced on 20th July 2015.

2015. Mody, Ashoka, *"Greece and the Andre Szasz Axiom "*, http://bruegel.org/2015/02/greece-and-the-andre-szasz-axiom-2/, sourced 24th February, 2015.

Monti, Mario, *A New Strategy for the Single Market*, European Commission, May, 2010.

Monnet, Jean, *Memories,* quotation sourced from speech by Stanley Fisher, Federal Reserve Governor, May 2015. www.federalreserve.gov/newevents/speech

Moore, Michael, *Doing Business Across Europe: A new engagement, Deputy Prime Minister's Office,* HMG, October 2014.

Mourlon-Druol, E, *"European leaders want the UK to stay"*, www.bruegel.org, sourced on 21 May, 2015.

Munchau, Wolfgang, "The wacky economics of Germany's parallel universe" in the *Financial Times, 16 November, 2014.*

Open Europe, *An eleven point mandate for the next European Commission,* Open Europe Briefing Paper, 8th September, 2014.

Open Europe, comments on European Parliament scrutiny of Commissioner candidates, www.openeurope.org.uk , sourced on 3 October 2014.

Open Europe, statistics on error rate in EU spending, http://openeurope.org.uk/daily-shakeup/eurozone-officials-dash-greek-hopes-of-securing-e1-2bn-from-bailout-fund/, sourced on 3 February 2015.

Open Europe, *The EU Climate Change and Renewable Energy Package: Are we about to be locked into the wrong policy?,* Open Europe, London, 2008.

Open Europe, *"Top 100 EU rules cost £33.3bn"*, www.openeurope.org.uk.

Pancevski, Bojan, "German invasion cuts Britons out of top Brussels jobs" in *Sunday Times,* 24 November, 2013.

Paterson, Owen, *An optimistic vision of a post EU United Kingdom*, http://www.uk2020.org.uk/wp-content/uploads/2014/10/Owen-Paterson-Europe-Speech-24-November-2014-Online.pdf.

PwC, *Public procurement in Europe, a study for the European Union,* PwC, 2011.

Philpott, Tim, *7% or 75%. The EU's influence over British Law: The definitive answer,* Business for Britain, London, 2015.

Pickard, Jim, "Britons split on EU exit, says poll" in the *Financial Times, 15 April, 2015.*

Pope Francis, speech to European Parliament, November 2014, http://www.catholicherald.co.uk/news/2014/11/25/pope-franciss-address-to-the-european-parliament-in-full/, Sourced on 13 August 2015.

Rachman, Gideon, "The West has lost its intellectual self confidence" in the *Financial Times,* 6 January, 2015.

Ridley, Matt, "A precautionary ban has made things worse for bees " in *The Times*, 13 October 2014.

Rigby, Elizabeth, "EU migrants to UK balanced by British living abroad " in the *Financial Times,* 10 February 2014.

Schwab, Klaus et al, *The Global Competitiveness Report 2013-14,* World Economic Forum, Geneva, 2013.

Sergie, Mohammed Ali, *"NAFTA's economic impact"*, Council on Foreign Relations, CFR Backgrounders, www.cfr.org.

Spiegel, Peter, " Draghi's ECB Management: the leaked Geithner files" in the *Financial Times,* 11 November, 2014.

Springford, John et al, *The Economic Consequences of leaving the EU,* Centre for European Reform, London, June 2014.

Stark, Jurgen, "The historical and cultural differences that divide Europe's Union" in the *Financial Times,* 12 February, 2015.

Stewart-Brown, Ronald*, "Discussion paper-UK Trade Statistics October 2013",* www.tprc.org.uk, sourced 15 Decemer 2014

TheCityUK, *Key facts about UK financial and professional services,* TheCityUK, January, 2014.

Thatcher, Margaret, *The Downing Street Years,* HarperCollins, London, 1993.

Timmermans, Frans, quoted in Euroobsever, https:// euobsever.com, sourced 3rd February 2015.

Tombs, Robert (ed), *European Demos, a historical myth?,* Business for Britain,London, 2014.

Traynor, Ian, "30,000 lobyists and counting " in *The Guardian,* 8 May, 2014.

Urwin, Derek, *The Community of Europe,* Routledge, London, 1964.

Webster, Ben & Devlin, Hannah, "Safety first rulings are stifling innovation ", *The Times*, 20 November, 2014.

Wood, Karen, *The World in 2050,* HSBC Global Research, London, January, 2012.

Wilson, Nigel, "One sided debate on Europe could force unnecessary Brexit " in *Daily Telegraph, 29 November 2014.*